Meaning by All Means

MEANING by ALL MEANS

A Vocabulary Text
and Workbook
for Students of ESL

CHARLES MASON
University of Hawaii

Prentice Hall Regents, Englewood Cliffs, NJ 07632

Library of Congress Cataloging-in-Publication Data

Mason, Charles (date)
  Meaning by all means.

    1. English language—Text-books for foreign
speakers. 2. Vocabulary. I. Title.
PE1128.M353 1986   428.1   85–16881
ISBN 0-13-567058-6

Editorial/production supervision
  and interior design: Joan L. Stone
Cover design: Lundgren Graphics, Ltd.
Manufacturing buyer: Harry P. Baisley

Printed in the United States of America

10 9 8 7 6 5

ISBN 0-13-567058-6 01

PRENTICE-HALL INTERNATIONAL (UK) LIMITED, *London*
PRENTICE-HALL OF AUSTRALIA PTY. LIMITED, *Sydney*
PRENTICE-HALL CANADA INC., *Toronto*
PRENTICE-HALL HISPANOAMERICANA, S.A., *Mexico*
PRENTICE-HALL OF INDIA PRIVATE LIMITED, *New Delhi*
PRENTICE-HALL OF JAPAN, INC., *Tokyo*
PRENTICE-HALL OF SOUTHEAST ASIA PTE. LTD., *Singapore*
EDITORA PRENTICE-HALL DO BRASIL, LTDA., *Rio de Janeiro*
WHITEHALL BOOKS LIMITED, *Wellington, New Zealand*

Contents

Preface

Students of English as a second language need to gain mastery of the general vocabulary used frequently in textbooks of the basic, introductory courses across the academic disciplines at both the college and high school levels. This book provides strategies for acquiring vocabulary without the constant use of the dictionary—namely, by using context clues, associational techniques, and inferences: to get meaning by all means.

The vocabulary selected for study in these exercises comes from the American University Word List (AUWL), a list compiled by Jean Praninskas after a search of textbooks used in introductory courses in ten different academic disciplines at the American University in Beirut. Further selection from Praninskas' 507 base-word list was made by surveying the students in the English Language Institute of the University of Hawaii and choosing the words from the Praninskas list that were least familiar to them. Of the original AUWL of 507 base words and 840 derivations, 237 base words and 351 derivations are used in this book. These exercises have been field-tested with the same English Language Institute students, a high-intermediate ESL group, with an average Test of English as a Foreign Language (TOEFL) score of approximately 520.

Description and Procedures

With the exception of the practice lesson, each of the remaining fifteen lessons are built around 15 base words from the AUWL. Each lesson contains five exercises that develop different strategies for getting meanings for the base words and their derivations without making use of the dictionary:

A. Vocabulary in context
B. Analogies
C. Word forms: derivations
D. Word associations: collocations
E. Definitions and paraphrases

xercise *A* provides two sentences for each study word. The first sentence of the pair
a meaning of the study word through a context clue that is one of the following types:
ı, restatement, example, modifier, or inference. The second sentence of the pair is either
r false statement based upon the meaning derived from the first sentence. The student
must decide whether the second sentence is true or false and mark it accordingly. This exercise
is worked through individually by students in class and then checked with other students in
groups of four or five. The group discusses its choices and attempts to arrive at a consensus.

Exercise *B* is concerned with analogies that put the study word into one of nine different relationships: synonym, antonym, cause-effect, part-whole, association, degree, action-actor,
action-object, or grammatical. Again, as in Exercise *A*, students work the analogies in class individually and check answers in the group of four or five, looking for consensus.

Exercise *C* requires the completion of a derivation table in which the noun, verb, adjective, and adverb forms are partially spelled out. After the table is completed, the sentence
completion portion asks the student to fill in the correct derivational form in a sentence, which
again gives meaning clues from its context.

Exercise *D* is a collocation, or word association, exercise in which the base words are put
into subject-verb patterns to be matched with phrases below them to make grammatically and
semantically sound sentences. In this exercise the student should see the patterns of collocation
for various verbs: the kinds of objects they take, if any, and the kinds of prepositions they are
matched with. Finally, the student is asked to write sentences using the same verbs and following
the models already provided. This exercise is difficult in that it requires creative production.

Exercise *E*, the final exercise of each lesson, asks the student to recognize a paraphrase
or definition of each of the study words and to match them, thereby completing a kind of glossary for further study in preparation for a multiple-choice test of the words. The test is administered after every fourth lesson.

The practice lesson explains each exercise and procedure in detail and should be gone
over carefully with the students.

To the Student

The great amount of reading you are expected to do for school assignments will require you to read quickly, or at least with a variety of speeds. For much of your reading you won't have time to use the dictionary to look up every word you don't know. Often you can get the meaning of a reading passage without knowing every word in it. You can guess the meanings of many unknown words from the context—that is, the sentences of the passages in which the words are found. Good readers of both first and second languages make intelligent guesses as to the meanings of words. The use of context to make guesses is a strategy, or skill, good readers have developed.

Many of the same context strategies you use to get word meanings in your first language can be transferred to your reading of English as a second language. As you read this passage you are using your knowledge of English grammar and English word parts to help you determine the functions of words in sentences. For example, you know that a word ending in *-ation* is probably a noun and that a word beginning with *in-*, *im-*, or *non-* has a negative meaning. More important, as you read you use your general knowledge of the world and your special knowledge of the topic you are reading about to make sense of the passage and to guess the meanings of unfamiliar words in the text.

In the exercises that follow, you will be asked to use the context strategies and clues already mentioned and to work with another set of context signals: the information an author builds into the writing to help the reader get the message. Textbook writers, especially, use techniques that help the reader to use the total context to arrive at a meaning for an individual word. The exercises in this book will deal with the kinds of signals used most often by writers, signals that are defined in the practice lesson. In addition, you will be using your powers of association to work the exercises of each lesson and discuss them with your classmates.

Meaning by All Means

PRACTICE
LESSON

Each lesson is comprised of five exercises, designed to help you get the meanings of 15 important and useful base words and their derivations. You will find these words frequently in your academic reading. These exercises will sharpen your skills in building your English vocabulary without using the dictionary.

In the first exercise of each lesson, *Exercise A: Vocabulary in Context,* you will be given two sentences for each study word. Sentence *a* of each pair indicates the meaning of the italicized study word through a context clue. There are five types of clues. Sentence *b* of the pair may be either true or false according to the meaning developed in sentence *a*. You must mark sentence *b* true or false. The context clue used in the first sentence of each pair will be one of the five types that follow:

Definition

The most obvious kind of information a writer can supply is a simple definition of a word or term. Often the word is defined in a single sentence of this pattern: *X is Y.*

Example

The *bourgeois* of a society are the middle-class people who own and manage businesses.

Restatement

The restatement clue is closely related to definition; however, the pattern is not *X is Y* but rather a form that is not as obvious.

Examples

Two political parties may coalesce—that is, unite as a single party—when it appears that their objectives are similar.

In order to solve a difficult problem we often start with a *hypothesis.* In other words, we begin by trying to guess the solution.

The *stereotype* of the college professor, the picture of a gentle, absent-minded person, is a typical Hollywood character.

Example

An author often gives examples to explain the meaning of a word. These examples may be signalled by words or phrases like the following: *such as, for example,* or *like.*

Examples

Capitalists, for example, those who control the stock of large business corporations, usually invest in a variety of money-making plans.

The government recognizes the right of citizens to *litigate* against it, such as in lawsuits where it is clear that a citizen has been mistreated by the government.

Modifiers

Phrases, clauses, or single words used for description may help to explain an unfamiliar word.

Examples

A *molecule* of water, which is composed of two hydrogen atoms and one oxygen atom, is lighter than a molecule of salt.

The *liberal,* always open to new ideas, is frequently elected during difficult times when change seems necessary.

Evidence of a meteor landing on earth is a *fragment* that had broken off in space and crashed to the ground in Arizona, U.S.A.

Inference

Perhaps most of the time a reader is required to use inference—the ability to see logical relationships or connections between key words, phrases, and sentences, to get meanings of unknown words in reading passages. Inference reveals meaning when the readers use their experience, intelligence, and knowledge of the language. In short, the reader must "read between the lines." As you read the examples below, your ability to make inferences should tell you something about the meaning of the italicized words.

Examples

The average student has little time to spend on *metaphysics*; he or she cannot spend hours answering questions like "What is the meaning of the universe?"

The mental patients *oscillate* between extreme feelings. They move from wild happiness to tearful sadness within a short period of time. There is seldom a feeling between these two extremes.

Is the human being the only *rational* animal, or can monkeys and dolphins also make some use of intelligence?

The 12 italicized words in the example sentences, used to illustrate the use of context clues, will be the vocabulary for study in this practice lesson. The 12 words for study are listed in alphabetical order:

bourgeois	hypothesis	molecule
capitalist	liberal	oscillate
coalesce	litigate	rational
fragment	metaphysics	stereotype

Exercise A

VOCABULARY IN CONTEXT

In the pairs of sentences that follow, sentence *a* is a true sentence that should help you to determine the meaning of the study word. Read sentence *a* and sentence *b*; decide whether the second sentence is true or false and put an **X** in the box before sentence *b*.

1. a. The *bourgeois* of a society are the middle-class people who own and manage the society's businesses.

T ☐ F ☐   b. A person who owns a small hat factory may be a *bourgeois*.

2. a. *Capitalists*, for example, those who control the stock of large business corporations, usually invest in a variety of money-making plans.

T ☐ F ☐   b. One might expect to find fewer *capitalists* in Russia than in Japan.

3. a. Two political parties may *coalesce*—that is, unite as a single party—when it appears that their objectives are similar.

T ☐ F ☐   b. The states of the United States have *coalesced*.

4. a. Evidence of a meteor landing on earth is a *fragment* that had broken off in space and crashed to the ground in Arizona, U.S.A.

T ☐ F ☐   b. At present we have only *fragments* of evidence that tell us about the history of humans on earth.

5. a. In order to solve a difficult problem we often start with a *hypothesis*, which is a kind of guess as to the solution.

T ☐ F ☐   b. It is only in dealing with scientific matters that it is necessary to make a *hypothesis*.

6. a. The *liberal*, always open to new ideas, is frequently elected during difficult times when change seems necessary.

T ☐ F ☐   b. *Liberals* are probably those people who like to live in the past.

7. a. The government recognizes the right of citizens to *litigate* against it, especially when citizens who have been mistreated by the government take legal action against it.

T ☐   F ☐   b. In a legal divorce action the husband or wife *litigates* against the other.

8. a. Average students feel that they have little time to spend on *metaphysics*; they cannot spend their hours answering questions like "What is the meaning of the universe?"

T ☐   F ☐   b. Philosophers are more likely than medical doctors to be concerned with *metaphysics*.

9. a. Two atoms of hydrogen and one atom of oxygen make up a single *molecule* of water, while one carbon atom and two oxygen atoms make up a single *molecule* of carbon dioxide.

T ☐   F ☐   b. It is likely that the characteristics of a substance are determined by the characteristics, or composition, of its *molecules*.

10. a. Some mental patients *oscillate* between extreme feelings. They move from wild happiness to tearful sadness within a short period of time.

T ☐   F ☐   b. The needle of the automobile speedometer *oscillates* as the car speeds up and slows down.

11. a. Are humans the only *rational* animals, or can monkeys and dolphins use their intelligence to make decisions?

T ☐   F ☐   b. The most *rational* approach to solving a problem is to try to forget it.

12. a. The *stereotype* of the college professor, the picture of a gentle, forgetful person, represents a typical Hollywood character.

T ☐   F ☐   b. No matter how accurate the *stereotype* for a group of people might be, there are always individuals in the group who do not fit the *stereotype*.

After you have completed *Exercise A*, join a group of four or five of your classmates to compare answers to the true-false statements. If you disagree with one another, try to explain why you answered the way you did. See if the group can agree whether the statement is true or false. Finally, the class as a whole should compare answers.

Exercise B
ANALOGIES

The second exercise in each lesson requires you to use your ability to see a relationship between words, to draw an analogy, and to apply this relationship to the study words of the lesson.

Analogies of nine types are used throughout the exercises in this book:

Synonym relationship:	Large is to big as happy is to glad.
Antonym relationship:	Tall is to short as good is to evil.
Part/whole relationship:	Wall is to house as arm is to body.
Association relationship:	Banker is to money as policeman is to crime.
	Teacher is to school as doctor is to hospital.
Degree relationship:	Warm is to hot as touch is to hit.
Action/actor relationship:	Sew is to tailor as write is to author.
Action/object relationship:	Bake is to bread as play is to game.

Cause/effect relationship: Hunger is to starvation as overwork is to tiredness.
Grammatical relationship: Inform is to information as perform is to performance.

Remember that the first pair of words in the analogy tells you what the relationship of the second pair of words will be. In the exercise that follows, pick a word from the list at the right to complete each analogy. Write the word in the blank provided. Two extra words in the list will *not* be used.

Analogies

1. Club is to member as molecule is to_____   attitude

2. Rhyme is to poetic as hypothesis is to_____   broken

3. Anatomy is to medicine as metaphysics is to_____   divide

4. Raise is to lower as coalesce is to_____   foolish

5. Calm is to violent as rational is to_____   guess

6. Artist is to sculpture as capitalist is to_____   join

7. Middle is to center as stereotype is to_____   lawyer

8. Cut is to injured as fragment is to_____   movement

9. Middle is to high as bourgeois is to_____   model

10. Hot is to temperature as liberal is to_____   investment

11. Noise is to sound as oscillate is to_____   atom

12. Command is to chief as litigate is to_____   philosophy

theoretical

royalty

Again, as you did in Exercise A, join a group of four or five of your classmates to compare answers to the analogies exercise.

Exercise C

WORD FORMS: DERIVATIONS

This exercise will help you become acquainted with the derivations, or words that can be formed from the study words (base forms) in the first two exercises. The form of the derivation indicates the grammatical function of the word. Learning the derivations along with the base forms helps you to increase your vocabulary three or four times as much.

Complete the following table by writing in the correct forms of the study words. Suffixes, the word endings, have been provided for you. The broken underline before each suffix indicates the number of letters you need to complete the derivation. Be sure to put a letter over each dash. Derivative forms that do not change from the base forms, and those that have an unusual spelling, have been spelled out for you over the dashes.

Noun Form	Verb Form	Adjective Form	Adverb Form
1. bourgeois		b o u r g e o i s	
_ _ _ _ _ _ _ _ ie			
2. capitalist		_ _ _ _ _ _ _ _ ic	
3. fragment	f r a g m e n t	_ _ _ _ _ _ _ ary	
_ _ _ _ _ _ _ ation			
4. hypothesis	_ _ _ _ _ _ _ ize	_ _ _ _ _ _ tical	_ _ _ _ _ _ _ _ _ _ lly
5. liberal	_ _ _ _ _ _ _ ize	l i b e r a l	_ _ _ _ _ _ _ ly
_ _ _ _ _ _ ization			
_ _ _ _ _ _ ism			
_ _ _ _ ation	_ _ _ _ _ ate		
_ _ _ _ _ ator			
6. _ _ _ _ _ ation	litigate		
7. metaphysics		_ _ _ _ _ _ _ _ _ al	_ _ _ _ _ _ _ _ _ _ _ ly
8. _ _ _ _ _ _ _ ence	coalesce		
9. molecule		_ _ _ _ _ _ _ ar	
10. _ _ _ _ _ _ _ tion	oscillate	_ _ _ _ _ _ _ _ ory	
11. _ _ _ _ _ _ _ _ ization	_ _ _ _ _ _ _ _ ize	rational	_ _ _ _ _ _ _ _ ly

You will use some of the word forms on this table to fill the blanks in the next exercise.

Sentence Completion

Use the table of derivative forms you have completed to fill the blanks in the next exercise. Use the noun, verb, adjective, or adverb form, depending upon the meaning of the sentence. The sentence numbers correspond to the numbers of the word groups in the table of derivations.

1. A _____ member of western society is quite common, especially in countries of Western Europe.

2. Western economic practices are probably best described as _____.

3. Breaking a glass object into many pieces is a good example of the process of _____ _____ .

4. Statements of scientists about the creation of the solar system are only _____ _____ statements.

5. The "Women's _____" movement around the world has changed the role of women in many countries.

6. Lawyers often earn high fees from _____ in which their clients sue large companies for great amounts of money.

7. _____ questions have been asked since human beings were first able to reason and to use language.

8. The _____ of all nations of the world seems quite unlikely at this time.

9. The _____ weight of water is different from that of alcohol.

10. The _____ of their wings enables birds to fly.

11. We hope to act _____ in times of extreme emergencies, such as fires or earthquakes.

Exercise D
WORD ASSOCIATIONS: COLLOCATIONS

"Knowing" a word means not only knowing a meaning for the word but also recognizing other words that are likely to be associated with it, recognizing the context in which the word might be found. This word association process is known as collocation.

In the exercise that follows, you are to associate the verbs from the study vocabulary with the clauses in the list provided. Fill in each blank with the subject-verb pattern that makes a complete, grammatical, and meaningful sentence. Write the *complete subject-verb pattern* in the blank, and use each subject-verb pattern at least once. (Some patterns complete more than one sentence.)

Subject-Verb Patterns

Men hypothesize	Electric current oscillates
Food buyers can litigate	A society can be fragmented
Mental patients often rationalize	Groups coalesce

1. _____ against improper price setting by businesses.
   against false claims in advertising.

2. _____ that space travel will become quite common.
   that Mars, the planet, cannot support life.

3. _____ their irregular behavior by blaming someone else.

4. _____ when unity works for their interests and for their safety.
   to gain stronger financial resources.

5. _____ by changing directions regularly.

6. _____ by war and hatred.
   by extreme differences in cultures within the same country.

Notice the kinds of words that immediately follow the verb and the kinds of sentence models that fit with certain verbs. You will use these sentence patterns or models to help you write sentences in the next exercise.

Words in Use

On the lines below write sentences of your own using the correct form of the verb in parentheses.

1. (hypothesize) _____

   _____

2. (litigate) _____

   _____

3. (oscillate) _____

   _____

4. (rationalize)_____

_____

5. (fragment)_____

_____

6. (coalesce)_____

_____

Exercise E

DEFINITIONS AND PARAPHRASES

Definitions and paraphrases are similar in function because both are used to explain meaning. Definitions are often shorter than paraphrases and more direct in explaining meaning. Paraphrases may be words, phrases, clauses, sentences, or whole passages written or spoken in words that are different from the original, but express the same general meaning. On the word level, for example, a synonym is a word-paraphrase that expresses a meaning similar to that of another word.

In the last exercise of each lesson, you are to complete phrases that form definitions or paraphrases of words studied in the lesson. You will be completing a kind of glossary or dictionary of the lesson words. After reading each of the incomplete phrases, select the correct word or word group from the vocabulary list and write it in the blank. Correct choices show that you understand the lesson vocabulary.

Words to Fill the Blanks

bourgeois	hypothesis	molecules
capitalists	liberal	oscillate
coalesce	litigate	rational
fragments	metaphysics	stereotype

1. The (study of _____), which looks for answers to questions about

what is real or unreal or about the meaning of life

2. The human quality of being (free-minded, willing to change, or _____)

3. To (move back and forth, shake, vibrate, or _____) like machine

parts in motion

4. The (bits, pieces, or _____) of a broken glass

5. A (middle-class, self-employed, or _____) member of a society

6. A (sensible, logical, reasonable, or _____) approach to a problem

7. To (take legal action, bring a lawsuit, sue, or _____) so that a court trial follows

8. A (fixed pattern of thinking, standard image, model, or _____) that develops in the mind

9. The (small units, particles, characteristic parts, or _____) of any material

10. A (belief, guess, theory, or _____) about a scientific experiment

11. To (combine, join forces, unite, or _____) with another company

12. The (wealthy persons, investors, money holders, or _____) who own major businesses

LESSON 1

Vocabulary

adhere	empirical	prosperous
aristocrat	enumerate	revolt
configuration	equate	segregate
correlate	kin	suffice
embryo	luster	transcend

Exercise A

VOCABULARY IN CONTEXT

Remember that to get the meaning of a word from context, you should look for a *definition*, a *restatement* of the term, *examples*, *modifiers*, or clues that allow you to make *inferences* about an unfamiliar word. The practice lesson provided examples of each of these five types of context clues. You may wish to look at those examples again.

In the following sentences, the first sentence of each pair, sentence *a*, gives you enough context to make a decision about a general meaning for the study word. After reading sentence *a*, decide whether sentence *b* is true or false. Mark your answer by putting an **X** in the *T* or *F* box before sentence *b*.

1. a. One who *adheres* strongly to the principles of democracy would respect the rights of others in the society.

T ☐ F ☐ b. A sure way to go to jail is to *adhere* to the laws.

2. a. The *aristocrats* of a society are generally those persons who are from the upper class because of their inherited wealth or positions.

T ☐ F ☐ b. In England, a member of the royal family would be called an *aristocrat*.

3. a. The clouds formed the *configuration* of a group of dancers, the outline of human shapes moving across the sky.

T ☐ F ☐ b. The *configuration* of an elephant makes it easy to identify.

4. a. The rate of plant growth *correlates* positively with the amount of rainfall in an area; that is, the increase or decrease of rain is followed by an increase or decrease in plant growth.

T ☐ F ☐ b. We would expect a positive *correlation* between height and weight in human beings.

11

   5. **a.** Once the *embryo* has formed in the female, it will grow into a fully developed human baby.

T ☐   F ☐   **b.** An *embryo* is a living thing.

   6. **a.** Practical scientists are *empirical* in their approaches to science, looking for answers by experimenting.

T ☐   F ☐   **b.** An *empirical* person is satisfied with theory and does not need evidence or proof of that theory.

   7. **a.** Counting the number of births within a country is a careful process; however, it is nearly impossible to *enumerate* all births.

T ☐   F ☐   **b.** The population of a place is determined by *enumerating* all living persons in that place, as closely as possible.

   8. **a.** Education cannot be *equated* with wisdom, nor can happiness be measured by wealth.

T ☐   F ☐   **b.** *Equating* things involves a comparison of some sort.

   9. **a.** Your parents and other *kin*, even your uncles and aunts, influence your life in some ways.

T ☐   F ☐   **b.** People generally marry their *kin*.

   10. **a.** The queen's crown of jewels shone with a *luster* like that of the noonday sun on the ocean.

T ☐   F ☐   **b.** Both silver and gold have *luster* when held in light.

   11. **a.** We all wish for a healthy body, a happy personality, a good mind, and a *prosperous*, or well-paying, form of work.

T ☐   F ☐   **b.** A *prosperous* business is one that makes money for its owner.

   12. **a.** Like the Americans in 1776, the French *revolted* against their form of government in 1789. Both countries were successful in becoming democracies.

T ☐   F ☐   **b.** People *revolt* most often when they are satisfied.

   13. **a.** Many schools still *segregate* males from females; in the past, universities enrolled only men.

T ☐   F ☐   **b.** Separation and *segregation* are similar in meaning.

   14. **a.** A well-chosen diet of 2400 calories should *suffice* to meet the needs of a 160-pound person in keeping regular body weight and good health.

T ☐   F ☐   **b.** If a person wakes up tired, her sleep has *sufficed*.

   15. **a.** Religion teaches us to rise above, to *transcend*, our everyday needs and desires in favor of deeper thoughts about our lives.

T ☐   F ☐   **b.** The value of owning an automobile *transcends* the value of an education.

Exercise B

ANALOGIES

Analogies of the types demonstrated in the practice lesson will be used in all the following analogy exercises. If you are uncertain of the kinds of relationships used in these analogies, look back at the practice lesson. Remember that the relationship of the words in the first pair tells you what the relationship should be for the words in the second pair.

From the list on the right, choose the word that completes the analogy. Write the word you have chosen in the blank. You will *not* use three of the 18 words in the list.

1. Busy is to **work** as **empirical** is to_____   revolution

2. Parent is to **father** as **kin** is to_____   animal

3. Push is to **shove** as **enumerate** is to_____   loyalty

4. Heavy is to **light** as **transcend** is to_____   give

5. Prince is to **farmer** as **aristocrat** is to_____   experience

6. Seed is to **plant** as **embryo** is to_____   uncle

7. Kill is to **death** as **revolt** is to_____   peasant

8. Neat is to **clean** as **prosperous** is to_____   shine

9. Brightness is to **glow** as **luster** is to_____   pretty

10. Heat is to **warmth** as **suffice** is to_____   combine

11. Separate is to **mix** as **segregate** is to_____   satisfaction

12. Talk is to **speak** as **correlate** is to_____   king

13. Equalize is to **balanced** as **equate** is to_____   count

14. Form is to **outline** as **configuration** is to_____   even

15. Enjoy is to **happiness** as **adhere** is to_____   fall short

pattern

successful

compare

Exercise C

WORD FORMS: DERIVATIONS

Complete the following table by writing the correct forms of the study words in the table. Suffixes, the word endings, have been provided for you. The broken underline before each suffix indicates the number of letters you need to complete the derivation. Be sure to put a letter over each dash. Derivative forms that do not change from the base forms, and those that have unusual spellings, have been spelled out for you over the dashes.

Noun Form	Verb Form	Adjective Form	Adverb Form
1. _ _ _ _ _ ence	adhere	_ _ _ _ _ ent	
_ _ _ _ _ ent			

Noun Form	Verb Form	Adjective Form	Adverb Form
2. aristocrat		_ _ _ _ _ _ _ _ ic	_ _ _ _ _ _ _ _ _ _ ally
_ _ _ _ _ _ _ _ cy			
3. _ _ _ _ _ _ tion	correlate		
4. _ _ _ _ _ _ ism		empirical	_ _ _ _ _ _ _ _ _ ly
5. _ _ _ _ _ _ tion	enumerate	_ _ _ _ _ _ _ _ ive	
6. _ _ _ _ tion	equate		
	_ _ _ _ lize		
7. luster		_ _ _ _ rous	
8. _ _ _ _ _ _ _ ity	p r o s p e r	prosperous	_ _ _ _ _ _ _ _ _ _ ly
9. _ _ _ _ _ ution	_ _ _ _ _ _ _ _ _ _ ize	_ _ _ _ _ _ _ _ _ ary	
	revolt		
10. _ _ _ _ _ _ _ _ ion	segregate		

Use words from this table to fill the blanks in the next exercise.

Sentence Completion

Use the table of derivative forms you have completed to fill the blanks in the following exercise. Choose the noun, verb, adjective, or adverb form, depending upon the meaning of the sentence. The sentence numbers correspond to the numbers of the word groups in the table.

1. _____ to the laws of a state or country is considered the duty of a

good citizen.

2. If a member of the royal family acts _____, no one is surprised.

3. We would expect to find a high, positive _____ between human intel-

ligence and vocabulary size.

4. When a decision is reached _____, the chances are that experience or experimentation has been involved.

5. The _____ ability of a child in counting from 1 to 100 is an ability that normal six-year-olds have developed.

6. The equal sign is an indication of an _____.

7. The _____ qualities of gold and diamonds make these materials attractive in jewelry.

8. Peace and security might result in a world that has overall economic _____

_____.

9. The idea that men could invent a machine that would allow them to fly was at one time considered _____.

10. A coeducational school is a school in which _____ of boys and girls is not the practice.

Exercise D

WORD ASSOCIATIONS: COLLOCATIONS

Choose subject-verb patterns from the following list to make complete, grammatical, and meaningful sentences. Write a *complete subject-verb pattern* in the blank before each word group. Some subject-verb patterns could be used to complete several sentences; however, each subject-verb pattern should be used at least once.

Subject-Verb Patterns

Researchers correlate   We try to equalize
We might segregate   Shopkeepers prosper
People sometimes revolt   Many people adhere

1. _____   in the business of selling hats.
   in good economic times.

2. _____   against a political system.
   against new social changes.

3. _____   to the principles of democracy.
   to the laws of a nation.
   to a policy of "first come, first served."

4. _____   student test scores with hours of study.
   income with years of education.

5. _____   diseased animals from healthy ones.
the sheep from the goats.

6. _____   the number of players on each team.
the supply of goods with the demand for them.

Notice the kinds of words that immediately follow the verb and the kinds of sentence models that fit with certain verbs. You will use these sentence patterns or models to write sentences of your own in the next exercise.

Words in Use

Write sentences of your own using the correct form of the verb given in parentheses.

1. (adhere)_____

_____

2. (equalize)_____

_____

3. (correlate)_____

_____

4. (prosper)_____

_____

5. (revolt)_____

_____

6. (segregate)_____

_____

Exercise E
DEFINITIONS AND PARAPHRASES

Complete a glossary of the lesson words. Read the incomplete phrases. Then select the correct word or word group from the vocabulary list and write it in the blank to complete each paraphrase or definition. Correct choices show that you understand the meanings of the vocabulary words.

Words to Fill the Blanks

adhere to	empirical	prosperous
aristocrat	enumerate	revolt against
configuration	equate	segregate
correlation	kin	suffice
embryo	luster	transcend

1. To (count, number, list or _____) objects, one by one

2. To (accept, follow, or _____) the customs of a society

3. To (separate, cut off, isolate, or _____) one group from another

4. To (oppose, fight against, _____) something you don't believe in

5. The (family, relatives, or _____) directly related to you

6. (A noble, a royal person, an upper-class person, an _____) in the social structure

7. To (compare, relate, connect, or _____) certain factors with one another

8. To (balance, even, or _____) numbers on both sides of the equal sign (=)

9. The (outline, form, pattern, or _____) of an object, such as a mountain seen in the distance

10. The word (_____), made up of a root word meaning *climb* or *rise* and a prefix meaning *over* or *above*

11. A (profitable, fortunate, successful, or _____) business

12. To (fulfill, satisfy, fill, or _____) basic human needs

13. The (shine, brightness, reflection, or _____) of diamonds

14. (A fertilized egg, a growing seed, or an _____) of a living organism

15. A (practical, experimental, experience-related, or _____) approach to a problem

LESSON

2

Vocabulary

annex	imperative	reign
confer	impulse	retain
dispute	morale	revive
ethnic	partition	sift
evolve	precede	torture

Exercise A

VOCABULARY IN CONTEXT

In the following sentences, sentence *a* gives you enough context to make a decision about a general meaning of the study word in the sentence. After reading sentence *a*, decide whether sentence *b* is true or false. Mark your answer by putting an **X** in the *T* or *F* box before sentence *b*.

1. a. The smaller building, built recently, is an *annex* of the larger building, connected by a long walkway.

T ☑ F ☐   **b.** The name Wist Hall *Annex* implies that there is an older building named Wist Hall.

2. a. Though the representatives of countries may *confer* for many days, their discussions rarely lead to complete agreement.

T ☑ F ☐   **b.** It takes at least two people to *confer*.

3. a. The *disputes* between employers and employees sometimes involve disagreements as to whether all employees must belong to a union.

T ☑ F ☐   **b.** A strike by workers is probably caused by a *dispute*.

4. a. An *ethnic* group is a large group of people who were born in the same nation or to the same race.

T ☑ F ☐   **b.** Members of an *ethnic* group are alike in some way.

19

5. a. Darwin's theories include the idea that present-day forms of life all *evolved* from earlier, simpler forms of life.

T ☑ F ☐   b. The jet airplane *evolved* from propeller-driven models.

6. a. Someone has said that two things are *imperative* for all people: to pay taxes and to die.

T ☐ F ☑   b. It is *imperative* for women to wear jewelry.

7. a. To avoid the *impulse* to buy unnecessary grocery items in the supermarket, don't shop when you are very hungry.

T ☑ F ☐   b. The ability of human beings to control *impulses* may be the most important factor in making humans "reasoning animals."

8. a. Psychologists find that the *morale* of college students is often low before final examinations and high after the tests; however, we would not expect everyone to be cheerful when final examinations are scheduled.

T ☐ F ☑   b. The happiest army is the one with the lowest *morale*.

9. a. The *partitions* separating one apartment from another in some new buildings are only thin sheets of cement.

T ☑ F ☐   b. *Partitions* have the function of dividing.

10. a. A good plan should *precede*, not follow, the growth of a large city.

T ☐ F ☑   b. In a single week Tuesday *precedes* Monday.

11. a. The *reign* of Queen Elizabeth I of England covered a period of 45 years, from 1558 to 1603.

T ☑ F ☐   b. *Reign* has about the same meaning as rule.

12. a. You can't *retain* your money and spend it at the same time.

T ☐ F ☑   b. The one who *retains* the title of "champion" in boxing has just lost a fight.

13. a. Fashion designers often *revive* the clothing styles of earlier generations but call these copies the "new look."

T ☐ F ☑   b. The sick person who *revives* is probably dead.

14. a. In order to find a small amount of gold, a miner must *sift* through tons of rock and sand.

T ☑ F ☐   b. *Sifting* could include separating smaller things from larger things.

15. a. Sometimes people are punished with great pain to make them confess to crimes. This process of *torture* is illegal in many places.

T ☐ F ☑   b. *Torture* always leads to death.

Exercise B

ANALOGIES

Choose a word from the list on the right to complete each analogy. Write the word you have chosen in the blank provided. You will *not* use three of the 18 words in the list.

1. **Difficult** is to **hard** as **imperative** is to _____*necessary*_____   group

2. **Sides** are to **triangle** as **partitions** are to _____*rooms*_____   necessary

3. **Happy** is to **sad** as **dispute** is to ___*agreement*___ ✓agreement

4. **Woman** is to **female** as **morale** is to ___*spirit*___ steal

5. **Listen** is to **concert** as **confer** is to ___*meeting*___ ✓spirit

6. **Permit** is to **allow** as **retain** is to ___*keep*___ ✓pain

7. **Close** is to **near** as **evolve** is to ___*develop*___ ✓king

8. **Happiness** is to **laughter** as **torture** is to ___*pain*___ terrible

9. **Small** is to **little** as **sift** is to ___*sort*___ ✓unconscious

10. **Lose** is to **find** as **precede** is to ___*follow*___ ✓reason

11. **Cake** is to **bake** as **annex** is to ___*connect*___ ✓sort

12. **Command** is to **general** as **reign** is to ___*king*___ swell

13. **Tall** is to **short** as **impulse** is to ___*reason*___ ✓connect

14. **Repair** is to **broken** as **revive** is to ___*unconscious*___ ✓develop

15. **Characteristic** is to **person** as **ethnic** is to ___*groups*___ ✓meeting

✓keep

✓follow

✓rooms

9:4

Exercise C

WORD FORMS: DERIVATIONS

Complete the following table by writing in the correct forms of the words already given. Suffixes, the word endings, have been provided for you. Broken underlines before each suffix indicate the number of letters you need to spell the correct, complete derivation. Be sure to put a letter over each dash. Derivative forms that do not change from the base forms, or that have unusual spellings, are written out over the dashes.

Noun Form	Verb Form	Adjective Form	Adverb Form
1. annex	a n n e x		
*annex*ation		*annexed*	—
2. *confer*ence	confer	*conferred*	—
3. dispute	d i s p u t e	disputable	disputably
		disputatious	

Noun Form	Verb Form	Adjective Form	Adverb Form
4. *ethnicity*	—	ethnic	*ethnic*ally
5. *evol*ution	evolve	*evolution*ary	
6. impulse	—	*impuls*ive	*impulsive*ly
7. partition	p a r t i t i o n	*partitioned*	—
8. *preced*ence *ent*	precede	*preceding*	—
9. reign	r e i g n	*reigning*	—
10. *retain*er *retention*	retain	*retaining*	—
11. *reviv*al	revive	*revived*	
12. *sift*er	sift	*sifted*	—
13. torture *tortur*er	t o r t u r e	*tortur*ous	*torturous*ly

Use the words from this table to fill the blanks in the next exercise.

Sentence Completion

Use the table of derivative forms you have completed to fill the blanks in the following exercise. Choose the noun, verb, adjective, or adverb form, depending upon the meaning of the sentence. The sentence numbers correspond to the numbers of the word groups in the table.

1. One country, usually a larger country, may ___*annex*___ a smaller one.

2. Diplomats often arrange ___*conferences*___ in Geneva, Switzerland, to discuss world problems.

3. A divorce is one way of ending a ___*dispute*___ *(argument)* between husband and wife.

4. A group of persons who speak the same language may be said to be ___*ethnically*___ *(classification of people by religion, language, culture, nationality — national origin)* related.

5. The universe is in a regular ___*evolutionary*___ process that may never end.
   (over a period of time)

6. The feeling of fear in humans and other animals may generally be considered a healthy
   ___*impulse*___ . *(w/o much thought)*

7. A room can be made larger or smaller if it is built with movable ___*partitions*___ .
   (separations)

8. In many cultures elderly citizens are given ___*precedence*___ in being allowed to
   (come first)
   enter doors before younger persons and take seats first.

9. In a good library quiet should ___*reign*___ . *(rule)*

10. When property is sold, the seller may write a contract that allows him ___*retention*___
    (to hold)
    _____ of minerals under the property.

11. A great ___*revival*___ of interest in learning and classic style took place in
    (new birth)
    Europe between 1300 and 1600. This period is known as the Renaissance.

12. A ___*sifter*___ is a very useful kitchen tool for separating flour into small
    (separator)
    grains.

13. A climb to the top of Mount Everest is a ___*torturous*___ experience for
    (painful)
    climbers.

Exercise D

WORD ASSOCIATIONS: COLLOCATIONS

Choose subject-verb patterns from the following list to make complete, grammatical, and meaningful sentences. Write a *complete subject-verb pattern* in each blank. Some subject-verb patterns can be used to complete several sentences; however, each subject-verb pattern should be used at least once.

Subject-Verb Patterns

They disputed	It evolved ②
We sifted	Let's partition
Someone might torture	You might precede
They annexed	They conferred
People often retain ①	She reigned
They revived	

1. _____   many memories of childhood.
   the good looks of their younger years.

2. _____   from a lower to a higher form of animal life.

3. _She reigned_ over her people for many years.
as beauty queen for a year.

4. _Let's partition_ the large room to make two small ones.

5. _We sifted_ the ruins of the fire to find our things.
the sand in search of shells.

6. _They disputed_ the right of employers to make employees work over-time.

7. _They revived_ the nearly drowned person.
the music of the past.

8. _They conferred_ with one another on the tax bill.
with other members of the legislature.

9. _You might precede_ someone through a door.

10. _Someone might torture_ prisoners to get them to say they are guilty.

11. _They annexed_ the new building to the old one.

Notice the kinds of words that immediately follow the verb and the kinds of sentence models that fit best with certain verbs. Use these sentence patterns or models to help you complete the next exercise.

Words in Use

Write sentences of your own using the correct form of the verb given in parentheses.

1. (dispute) _____

_____

2. (annex) _____

_____

3. (retain) _____

_____

4. (revive) _____

_____

5. (evolve) _____

_____

0. (precede)_____

_____

7. (confer)_____

_____

Exercise E
DEFINITIONS AND PARAPHRASES

Complete a glossary of the lesson words. Read the incomplete phrases in the following exercise. Then select the correct word from the vocabulary list and write it on the blank to complete each paraphrase or definition. Correct choices show that you understand the meanings of the words.

Words to Fill the Blanks

annex	imperative	reign
confer	impulse	retain
dispute	morale	revive
ethnic	partition	sift
evolve	precede	torture

1. (A fight, opposition, an argument, a _dispute_) because of disagreement

2. To (separate, examine, sort, or _sift_) the wreckage for evidence of the cause of the crash

3. To (meet, discuss, talk, _confer_) with others about plans for the future

4. (Punishment, pain, hurt, or _torture_) which could be of the mind or body

5. An (_ethnic_ group), which is related by race, language, or nationality

6. The (rule, administration, time in office, or _reign_) of a king or queen

7. An (_annex(ation)_), which is something connected, joined, or added to something else

8. A (separation, division, wall, or _partition_), that keeps rooms apart

9. (Required, necessary, compulsory, or _imperative_) events like eating or sleeping

10. To (bring to life, restore, regain the spirit of, or _____revive_____) a thing from the past

11. To (develop, change, progress, or _____evolve_____) as plants and animals do over many generations

12. The (urge, desire, feeling, or _____impulse_____) that drives one toward action

13. To (come before, come earlier, go ahead of, or _____precede_____) as one century does before another

14. Your (temper, spirit, state of mind, or _____morale_____), which helps you keep psychological balance

15. To (keep, hold, remember, or _____retain_____) an idea or a memory

LESSON 3

2:23 -

Vocabulary

assert	metropolis	premise
deduce	norm	sect
dense	parliament	skull
fuse	persist	subtle
instinct	precise	suppress

9:24 - 9:25

Exercise A

VOCABULARY IN CONTEXT

In the following sentences, sentence *a* gives you enough context to make a decision about a general meaning for the study word in the sentence. After reading sentence *a*, decide whether sentence *b* is true or false. Mark your answer by putting an **X** in the *T* or *F* box before sentence *b*.

1. a. When you take an oath in a court of law you *assert* that you will tell the truth.

   T ☒ F ☐ b. We expect that anything *asserted* has been communicated in some way.

2. a. From evidence already known and from new experiments, scientists can *deduce* solutions to problems.

   T ☒ F ☐ b. Before we *deduce* something, we have to think about it.

3. a. The clouds were so *dense* that the pilot could not see the ground.

   T ☒ F ☐ b. A large city has a *dense* population.

4. a. When copper and zinc are *fused*, or melted together, they form brass.

   T ☒ F ☐ b. Things that are *fused* are joined together.

5. a. Among the few *instincts*, or unlearned behaviors, found in mammals is the *instinct* to suck for food immediately after birth.

   T ☐ F ☒ b. *Instincts* require training in order to be used effectively.

6. a. New York City is the largest *metropolis* in the United States.

   T ☒ F ☐ b. You would be correct in referring to Tokyo as a *metropolis*.

7. a. Every culture sets the norms for the *behavior* of the people who live within that culture. Those who do not follow these rules may not be accepted by that society.

T ☑ F ☐   b. We expect the "average" person to follow the *norms* of a society.

8. a. The primary duty of members of a *parliament* is to make laws.

T ☑ F ☐   b. Work in a *parliament* is apparently a group activity.

9. a. After all these years, a story still *persists* that a real monster lives in Loch Ness in Scotland.

T ☐ F ☑   b. A disease that *persists* in the modern world is one that no longer exists.

10. a. The modern computer, the most *precise* instrument for making decisions in air navigation, is much more exact than the instruments of ten years ago.

T ☑ F ☐   b. Establishing the weight of an atom requires a *precise* measurement.

11. a. A sound theory is based upon a series of *premises*, or logical ideas, that support the theory.

T ☑ F ☐   b. A *premise* could be part of the evidence that someone gives to prove a point.

12. a. Hindus are the third largest religious *sect* in the world today.

T ☑ F ☐   b. It takes a group to form a *sect*.

13. a. The *skull* protects the brain, just as other bones of the body protect important organs.

T ☑ F ☑   b. An adult *skull* is about the size of an average apple.

14. a. Changes caused by the aging process in human beings are *subtle*, hardly noticeable from year to year.

T ☐ F ☑   b. The most *subtle* differences in meaning are the easiest to understand. *hardest*

15. a. Any attempt to *suppress* the news may also be an attempt to hide the truth.

T ☐ F ☑   b. Information that is *suppressed* is made available to everyone.

Exercise B

ANALOGIES

9:33 - 9:39

Choose a word from the list on the right to complete the analogy. Write the word you have chosen in the blank provided. You will *not* use three of the 18 words in the list on the right.

1. **Stupid** is to **dumb** as **precise** is to _exact_   congress

2. **License** is to **permit** as **norm** is to _standard_   theory

3. **Forest** is to **woods** as **parliament** is to _Congress_   defend

4. **Repair** is to **fix** as **assert** is to _announce_   continue

5. **Team** is to **players** as **sect** is to _followers_   uncover

6. **Come** is to **go** as **fuse** is to _separate_   mind

7. Puzzle is to problem as metropolis is to _city_____ ✓skeleton

8. Choose is to pick as persist is to _continue_____ separate

9. Taste is to mouth as deduce is to _mind_____ heat

10. Smart is to intelligent as subtle is to _indirect_____ ✓announce

11. Leg is to body as skull is to _skeleton_____ thick

12. Give is to take as suppress is to _announce_____ ✓city

13. Piece is to whole as premise is to _theory_____ select

14. Itch is to scratching as instinct is to _behaving_____ behaving

15. Grateful is to thankful as dense is to _thick_____ ✓followers

✓exact

✓indirect

✓standard

Exercise C
WORD FORMS: DERIVATIONS

Complete the following table by writing in the correct forms of the study words. Suffixes, the word endings, have been provided for you. The broken underline before each suffix indicates the number of letters you need to spell the correct, complete derivation. Be sure to put a letter over each dash. Derivative forms that do not change from the base forms, or that have unusual spellings, are written out for you over the dashes.

Noun Form	Verb Form	Adjective Form	Adverb Form
1. assertion	assert	assertive	assertively
2. deduction	deduce	deductive	deductively
3. density		dense	densely
4. fusion	fuse		
5. instinct		instinctive	instinctively
6. metropolis		metropolitan	
7. norm	normalize	normal	normally

Noun Form	Verb Form	Adjective Form	Adverb Form
8. parliament		parliamentary	
9. persistence	persist	persistent	persistently
10. precision		precise	precisely
11. sect		sectarian	
12. subtlety / subtleness	subtle	_discriminating, crafty, clever, thin, rare – making fine distinctions_	subtly
13. suppression	suppress	suppressive	suppressively

Use words from this table to fill the blanks in the next exercise.

Sentence Completion

Use the table of derivative forms you have completed to fill the blanks in the following exercise. Use the noun, verb, adjective, or adverb form, depending upon the meaning of the sentence. The sentence numbers correspond to the numbers of the word groups in the table.

1. We might expect someone who is not guilty of a crime to state _assertively_ _(persistently)_ that she is not guilty.

2. To arrive at an answer to a question _deductively_, one must start with some known facts.

3. Hong Kong is more _densely_ populated than Honolulu.

4. It takes great heat to bring about the _fusion_ of some metals; others can be joined with much less heat.

5. In the study of human behavior, scientists are still not clear what is learned behavior and what is _instinctive_ behavior.

6. One of the major problems in most large _metropolitan_ areas is the difficulty in controlling traffic.

7. What is _____ *normal* _____ behavior in one society may be quite unusual in another society.

8. Most organizations hold business meetings under the direction of a set of _____ *parliamentary* _____ rules, which keep the meetings orderly.

9. The _____ *persistence* _____ of fog in some areas of the world can keep airplanes from landing and taking off on regular schedules.

10. Computers are now being used to assist in the navigation of complex, high-speed jetliners because speed and _____ *precision* _____ are required in making decisions.

11. Within Christianity itself there are many _____ *sectarian* _____ groups whose beliefs differ greatly from one another's.
    (narrow minded) holding the same set of opinions or beliefs

12. When you wish to ask someone to do a favor for you without giving a direct order, a hint or suggestion is a more _____ *subtle* _____ way of asking.

13. In most societies human beings accept a certain amount of _____ *suppression* _____ of their individual desires so that the society can function for the good of all.

Exercise D   *Hwuck.*

WORD ASSOCIATIONS: COLLOCATIONS

Choose the subject-verb patterns from the list to make complete, grammatical, and meaningful sentences. Write a *complete subject-verb pattern* in the blank before each word group. Some subject-verb patterns can be used to complete several sentences; however, each subject-verb pattern should be used at least once.

Subject-Verb Patterns

You might suppress   You may deduce
The boy asserted   We can fuse
They persist   Medication can normalize

1. _____ *We can fuse* _____ platinum and gold to make a ring.

2. _____ *You might suppress* _____ the freedom of speech of a group.
   your guilty feelings by forgetting.

3. _____ *You may deduce* _____ the answer to a puzzle.
   several solutions to a problem.

4. _The boys asserted_   that he was going to quit school.
                               that he was ready to get married.

5. _Educator can normalize_   the unusual behavior of some people.

6. _They persist_   in the idea of winning the game.
                               in their efforts to become famous.

Notice the kinds of words that immediately follow the verb and the kinds of sentence models that fit with certain verbs. You will use these sentence patterns or models to help you write sentences of your own in the next exercise.

Words in Use

Write sentences of your own using the correct form of the verb given in parentheses.

1. (suppress) _____

   _____

2. (assert) _____

   _____

3. (persist) _____

   _____

4. (deduce) _____

   _____

5. (fuse) _____

   _____

6. (normalize) _____

   _____

Exercise E
DEFINITIONS AND PARAPHRASES

Complete a glossary of the lesson words. Read the incomplete phrases in this exercise. Then select the correct word or word group from the vocabulary list and write it in the blank to complete each paraphrase or definition. Correct choices show that you understand the meanings of the words of the lesson.

Words to Fill the Blanks

assert ✓	metropolis ✓	premise ✓
deduce ✓	norm	sect ✓
dense	parliament ✓	skull ✓
fuse ✓	persist in ✓	subtle ✓
instinct ✓	precise ✓	suppress ✓

1. (A piece of evidence, an idea, a point, a ___premise___) used in a scientific theory or legal argument

2. To (decide, reason, figure out, ___deduce___) answers to questions that require much thought

3. The (headbone, brain container, skeleton part, ___skull___) functioning for the body's protection

4. To (continue, hang on to, keep going with, ___persist in___) a belief or habit

5. A (population center, city, cultural center, ___metropolis___) like Paris, France

6. (An exact, a careful, a very fine, a ___precise___) scientific measurement

7. An insult that is (hard to understand, hard to see, indirect, ___subtle___)

8. A (social group, group of believers, group of followers, ___sect___) with similar interests

9. To (say, announce, insist upon, ___assert___) what you believe in

10. (An urge, a feeling, an unlearned behavior, an ___instinct___) that we see in many animals

11. To (mix, blend, bring together, ___fuse___) several metals

12. A (congress, lawmaking body, governing body, ___parliament___) found in many democratic countries

13. To (stop, prevent, hold back, ___suppress___) the flow of news

14. The (standard, model, average, ___norm___) for a cultural group

15. A (thick, heavy, concentrated, ___dense___) layer of fog

LESSON 4

Vocabulary

arouse ‿	err ‿	prevail
cease ‿	gene ‿	proclaim ‾
condense ‿	infer ‾	rebel ‿
contrary ‿	momentum ‾	regime ‿
emit	parasite ‿	revise ‾

Exercise A

VOCABULARY IN CONTEXT

In the sentences below, the first sentence in each pair, sentence *a*, gives you enough context to make a decision about a general meaning for the lesson word in the sentence. After reading sentence *a*, decide whether sentence *b* is true or false. Mark your answer by putting an **X** in the *T* or *F* box before sentence *b*.

1. a. The purpose of advertising is to *arouse* feelings of need for the advertised product.

T ☑ F ☐   b. When persons are happy, sad, or angry, their emotions are *aroused*. *to stir up*

2. a. Death is defined as that point at which both the heart and the brain have *ceased* to function. *stop*

T ☐ F ☑   b. We *ceased* using the automobile as a means of transportation about 1900.

3. a. Some magazines *condense* longer articles from other magazines so that readers can get the idea of the articles without spending a great deal of time reading. *make smaller, reduce*

T ☑ F ☐   b. Taking lecture notes is a way of *condensing* a one-hour lecture.

4. a. The careful scientist does not believe statements that are *contrary* to evidence or facts. *against, opposed, differ*

T ☑ F ☐   b. Rain coming down from a clear blue sky is *contrary* to what you would expect.

5. a. Some elements *emit* energy that, like the rays of the sun, can be either good or harmful to humans. *give off, to send out, issue*

T ☑ F ☐   b. A scream can be *emitted* from a frightened child.

6. a. All humans *err* during their lives, but they also learn from their mistakes.

T ☑ F ☐   b. It is possible to *err* by being too cautious. *make mistake, to be wrong*

7. a. Human characteristics such as hair color and eye color are carried by *genes* from parents to child. *elements by which hereditary characteristics are transmitted*

T ☑ F ☐   b. The study of *genes* is a branch of biology.

8. a. If the sky is full of dark clouds, you can *infer* that rain may fall. *(something else unseen) conclude, deduce*

T ☐ F ☑   b. Before you can *infer* something, you must prove it.

9. a. *Momentum* is the force with which a body moves. A faster moving body will produce more *momentum* than a slower moving one.

T ☐ F ☑   b. A piano sitting on a floor has *momentum*.

10. a. Plants and animals that live in or on the bodies of other living things without providing any support to their hosts are known as *parasites*.

T ☑ F ☐   b. Healthy adult humans who live at others' expense without paying back might also be called "*parasites*." *to exist widely*

11. a. The trade winds *prevail* over the Hawaiian Islands, but on the few days when the trades are not blowing, the wind may come from the opposite direction.

T ☑ F ☐   b. Something that *prevails* in a place is quite common there. *stated or announced formally*

12. a. The man *proclaimed* his innocence, and the jury believed his statement.

T ☑ F ☐   b. *To proclaim* and *to keep secret* are opposite in meaning.

13. a. Not every *rebel* carries a gun; some simply disagree with the rules of their society by acting differently.

T ☐ F ☑   b. *Rebels* were unknown before the twentieth century. *① political system ② social system ③ course of history*

14. a. A communist *regime* has been governing China since 1949.

T ☑ F ☐   b. The present *regime* in any country is the government now in power. *(those) bring up to date*

15. a. The job of the news editor is to *revise* what is written by reporters whenever there is a need for correction or change.

T ☑ F ☐   b. The second edition of a book is probably a *revised* edition.

Exercise B

ANALOGIES

Choose a word from the list on the right to complete each analogy. Write the word you have chosen in the blank provided. You will *not* use three of the 18 words in the list on the right.

1. **Force** is to **explosion** as **momentum** is to _____movement_____   ✓idea

2. **Flow** is to **liquid** as **emit** is to _____sound_____   ✓movement

3. **Murder** is to **killed** as **condense** is to _____shortened_____   ✓announcement

4. **Destroy** is to **ruined** as **err** is to _____mistaken_____   _opposite

5. **Nation** is to **Thailand** as **regime** is to _____Communism_____   ✓agreeable

6. **Think** is to **thought** as **proclaim** is to _announcement_   ✓rebellion

7. **Fire** is to **heat** as **genes** is to _characteristics_   ✓characteristics

8. **Musician** is to **music** as **rebel** is to _rebellion_   choice

9. **Climate** is to **weather** as **revise** is to _change_   sound

10. **Transportation** is to **airplane** as **parasites** is to _fleas_   ✓shortened

11. **Manufacture** is to **product** as **infer** is to _idea_   ✓mistaken

12. **Search** is to **discovery** as **arouse** is to _emotion_   stop

13. **Divorce** is to **marry** as **cease** is to _begin_   ✓fleas

14. **Exhausted** is to **refreshed** as **contrary** is to _agreeable_   ✓begin

15. **Exist** is to **people** as **prevail** is to _customs_   ✓customs

✓change

✓emotion

✓Communism

Exercise C

WORD FORMS: DERIVATIONS

Complete the following table by writing in the correct forms of the words already given. Suffixes, or word endings, have been provided for you. The broken underline before a suffix indicates the number of letters you need to spell the correct, complete derivation. Be sure to put a letter over each dash. Derivative forms that do not change from the base forms, and those that have unusual spellings, are written out for you over the dashes.

Noun Form	Verb Form	Adjective Form	Adverb Form
1. arousal	arouse		
2. cessation	cease		
3. condensation	condense		
4. emission	emit		
5. error	err	erroneous	
		erratic	erratically

Noun Form	Verb Form	Adjective Form	Adverb Form
6. gene		_gene_tic	_genetic_ally
7. _infer_ence	infer	_infer_ential	
8. parasite		_parasit_ic	
9. _prevalence_	prevail	_prev_alent	
10. _proclamation_	proclaim		
11. rebel	_rebel_	_rebel_lious	
_rebel_lion			
12. _revis_ion	revise		

Use the words from this table to fill the blanks in the next exercise.

Sentence Completion

Use the table of derivative forms you have completed to fill the blanks in the following exercise. Use the noun, verb, adjective, or adverb form, depending upon the meaning of the sentence. The sentence numbers correspond to the numbers of the word groups in the table.

1. The _____arousal_____ of fear or anger in a human being often brings an increased blood flow to the face.

2. The _____cessation_____ of war is brought about by a treaty, or agreement, signed by the opposing military forces.

3. We would expect the _____condensation_____ of a book to be shorter than the original book.

4. One of the great dangers in the use of nuclear power is the accidental _____emission_____ _____ of radioactive gases.

5. While banks often make mistakes in their procedures, customers have the right to expect bankers to find _____erroneous_____ calculations and correct them.

6. While intelligence seems to be primarily __*genetic*__ in origin, environment also appears to affect intelligence.

7. __*Inferences*__ about the character of a person are often made incorrectly from the person's appearance.

8. Where public health is not considered important, or where it is nearly impossible to maintain, we might find a number of __*parasitic*__ diseases.

9. Only desert plants are __*prevalent*__ in an area where rainfall is scarce and temperatures are extreme.

10. Holidays may come into being by the __*proclamation*__ of a legislature or the head of a government.

11. Teenage children appear to develop __*rebellious*__ characteristics when they are attempting to become independent of the parents and the home.

12. School textbooks are often __*revisions*__ of earlier editions.

Exercise D
WORD ASSOCIATIONS: COLLOCATIONS

Choose subject-verb patterns from the list to make complete, grammatical, and meaningful sentences. Write a *complete subject-verb pattern* in each blank. Some subject-verb patterns could be used to complete several sentences; however, each subject-verb pattern should be used at least once.

Subject-Verb Patterns

The speech aroused
The workers ceased
The researchers condensed
The compound emits
The investor erred

She infers
The animal prevails
The order proclaimed
The party members rebelled
The author revised

1. __*The workers ceased*__   all activity for one day.
   operations in the factory.

2. __*She infers*__   that her salary will be raised this week.
   from his appearance that he is unhappy.

3. __*The investor erred*__   in thinking that he couldn't lose money.
   in making the financial decision.

4. _The author revised_ many sentences in his story.
all chapters of an earlier book.

5. _The compound emits_ rays that are dangerous.
gas when it is heated.

6. _The order proclaimed_ next Friday as a state holiday.
Charles as King of England.

7. _The animal prevails_ in environments with very little rain.
in subtropical climates.

8. _The party members rebelled_ against the existing form of government.
against the suggestion to change the law.

9. _The speech aroused_ pity for the hungry people.
the emotions of the audience.

10. _The researchers condensed_ steam back to liquid.
the process from 2 hours to 1 hour.

Notice the kinds of words that immediately follow the verb and the kinds of sentence models that fit with certain verbs. You will use these sentence patterns or models to help you write sentences in the next exercise.

Words in Use

Write sentences of your own using the correct form of the verb in parentheses.

1. (arouse) _____

_____

2. (cease) _____

_____

3. (emit) _____

_____

4. (infer) _____

_____

5. (prevail) _____

_____

6. (proclaim)_____

_____

7. (rebel)_____

_____

8. (revise)_____

_____

Exercise E

DEFINITIONS AND PARAPHRASES   *[handwritten]*

Complete a glossary of the lesson words. Read the incomplete phrases in this exercise. Then select the correct word or word group from the vocabulary list and write it in the blank to complete each paraphrase or definition. Correct choices show that you understand the meanings of the words of the lesson.

Words to Fill the Blanks

arouse	err	prevail
cease	gene	proclaim
condense	infer	rebel
contrary to	momentum	regime
emit	parasite	revise

1. To (announce, state publicly, declare, _proclaim_) a new law

2. The (force, movement, pressure, _momentum_) of a pushed object

3. The (government, management, system, _regime_) of a political party in office

4. A happening (opposite to, unfavorable to, not in agreement with, _contrary to_ _____) the laws of nature

5. To (reason, decide, understand, _infer_) from the data or evidence

6. A (_rebel_) who opposes, fights against, revolts against the existing government

7. A (unit of heredity, developmental factor, characteristic determiner, _gene_) given from parent to child

8. To (release, send out, discharge, _____emit_____) a dangerous gas

9. To (thicken, reduce, concentrate, _____condense_____) a mixture by boiling

10. To (make a mistake, do wrong, be wrong, _____err_____) in your behavior

11. To (stop, discontinue, end, _____cease_____) an activity

12. A (_____parasite_____), which depends upon, lives on, or eats from another organism

13. To (exist, dominate, be common, _____prevail_____) in a certain area or climate

14. To (review, re-examine, correct, _____revise_____) a research paper

15. To (stimulate, excite, stir up, _____arouse_____) emotions or feelings

LESSON 5

Vocabulary

antithesis	conceive	nebulous
attain	denounce	reveal
census	divine	secular
clot	filament	spontaneous
commune	investigate	sustain

Exercise A

VOCABULARY IN CONTEXT

In the sentences below, the first sentence in each pair, sentence *a*, gives you enough context so that you can make a decision about a general meaning for the study word in the sentence. After reading sentence *a*, decide whether sentence *b* is true or false. Mark your answer by putting an **X** in the *T* or *F* box before sentence *b*.

1. a. Love is the *antithesis* of hate. *opposite*

T ☐ F ☑   b. The *antithesis* of unhappiness is sadness.

2. a. Earning a university degree means that you have *attained* one objective in your total life goals.

T ☐ F ☑   b. Most people have *attained* their major goals in life by the time they reach *to reach* legal age.

3. a. The United States *census* of 1980 showed a population count of around 240 million. *# count*

T ☑ F ☐   b. A report of the number of Hindus in a certain nation is a kind of *census*.

4. a. If a blood *clot* blocks a major blood vessel in the brain, the result may be paralysis or even death. *Coagulate, to become hard*

T ☑ F ☐   b. Apparently *clots* are formed by some hardening process.

5. a. It is said that poets are able to *commune* with nature and that poems are the messages nature gives them. *to partake, communicate* *to think, ponder w/ oneself*

T ☑ F ☐   b. Certain gifted people may *commune* with the spirit world.

43

6. a. What Einstein *conceived* was a new look at the very old laws of nature.

T ☑ F ☐   b. A person can *conceive* an idea. *to think up*

7. a. Many of the world's greatest thinkers were at first *denounced* as insane by others in their societies.

T ☐ F ☑   b. Studying hard for examinations is *denounced* by most university professors. *condemn, criticize*

8. a. Humans are capable of *divine* thought, that which is worthy of the gods.

T ☑ F ☐   b. "Heavenly" and *divine* are similar in meaning.

9. a. What lights an electric bulb is a *filament* that heats up within the bulb. When this thin wire breaks, the bulb "burns out."

T ☑ F ☐   b. A spider's web is a series of *filaments*. — *slender thread or fibre*

10. a. Scientists are *investigating* the planet Saturn with instruments that now show the planet's surface and rings in much greater detail.

T ☑ F ☐   b. A university thesis, or research paper, describes an *investigation*. *careful search, examination*

11. a. Instead of the *nebulous* promises politicians make at election time, voters should demand clear, easily understood statements of realistic goals.

T ☐ F ☑   b. The clearest explanation must also be the most *nebulous*. *cloudy, misty*

12. a. The microscope *reveals* many forms of life that can't be seen with the eyes alone. *to show, to expose to view, display*

T ☑ F ☐   b. Something *revealed* has been sensed in some way. *to become aware of, to comprehend, understand*

13. a. Members of both the *secular* and the religious communities should take part in political affairs.

T ☐ F ☑   b. A priest or monk is a *secular* person. *belonging to the world, layman*

14. a. Body responses such as breathing and heart beats are *spontaneous* functions, completely automatic for the most part.

T ☑ F ☐   b. A sneeze is a *spontaneous* action.

15. a. The oxygen the astronauts carried with them to the moon would have *sustained* them for more than a week after their planned return date.

T ☑ F ☐   b. Water is necessary to *sustain* life. *support*

Exercise B

ANALOGIES

Choose a word from the list on the right to complete the analogy. Write the word in the blank provided. You will *not* use three of the 18 words in the list.

1. Study is to know as investigate is to ____*find*____   life

2. Maintain is to property as sustain is to ____*life*____   change

3. Rock is to stone as clot is to ____*lump*____   find

4. Book is to education as census is to ____*population*____   idea

5. Flower is to rose as filament is to ____*hair*____   communication

6. Remember is to forget as denounce is to _praise_ — lump

7. Quantity is to measurement as antithesis is to _contrast_ — division

8. Complete is to finish as attain is to _get_ ✓population

9. Tell is to hear as reveal is to _see_ ✓saint

10. Beautiful is to movie actress as divine is to _saint_ — selection

11. Quick is to slow as spontaneous is to _planned_ ✓get

12. Pleasant is to pleased as nebulous is to _uncertain_ ✓see

13. Build is to house as conceive is to _idea_ ✓religious

14. Fat is to thin as secular is to _religious_ ✓uncertain

15. Pay is to payment as commune is to _Communication_ ✓planned

✓hair

✓praise

✓contrast

Exercise C

WORD FORMS: DERIVATIONS

Complete the following table by writing in the correct forms of the study words. Suffixes have been provided for you. A broken underline before each suffix indicates the number of letters you need to spell the correct, complete derivation. Be sure to put a letter over each dash. Derivative forms that do not change from the base forms, and those that have unusual spellings, are written out for you over the dashes.

Noun Form	Verb Form	Adjective Form	Adverb Form
1. _attain_ment	attain		
2. clot	_clot_	_clot_ table	
3. _commune_	commune	_commun_ al	
commun ity			
commun ication	_commun_ icate	_communicat_ ive	
4. _conception_	conceive	_conceiv_ able	_conceivab_ ly
concept		_concept_ ual	_conceptual_ ly

Noun Form	Verb Form	Adjective Form	Adverb Form
5. d e n u n c i a t i o n	denounce		
6. _divin_ity		divine	_divine_ly
7. _investigat_ion	investigate	_investigat_ive	
8. r e v e l a t i o n	reveal		
9.		spontaneous	_spontaneous_ly
10. s u s t e n a n c e	sustain		

Use words from this table to fill the blanks in the next exercise.

Sentence Completion

Use the table of derivative forms you have completed to fill the blanks in this exercise. Use the noun, verb, adjective, or adverb form, depending upon the meaning of the sentence. The sentence numbers correspond to the numbers of the word groups in the table.

1. The ____attainment____ of a university degree or diploma certainly should not be the end of a person's education.

2. Blood will ____clot____ very quickly when it is exposed to air.

3. People who live together in a ____commune____ probably have similar interests or are alike in some way.

4. The ____conceptual____ power of human beings is seen in our ability to think about the world with symbols like language.

5. Newspaper editorials often ____denounce____ the activities of crooked politicians who accept money for favors.

6. Christ and Buddha are considered ____divine____ by their followers.

7. The ____investigative____ powers of the police in our society are limited by a law that requires them to have a written order to search a home.

8. Very creative people can often get a new idea in the form of a _____revelation_____, which comes to them like a dream during sleep.

9. Fire can start _____spontaneously_____ if the conditions are just right.

10. We depend upon a supply of air, water, and food for the _____sustenance_____ of life.

Exercise D

WORD ASSOCIATIONS: COLLOCATIONS

Choose subject-verb patterns from the list to make complete, grammatical, and meaning-ful sentences. Write a *complete subject-verb pattern* in the blank before each word group. Each subject-verb pattern should be used.

Subject-Verb Patterns

You may attain
The mixture will clot
An unusual person may commune
He conceived

You might denounce
She could be investigating
They revealed
The company can sustain

1. ___He conceived___ a new plan for making money.
   the idea of the gasoline engine.

2. ___The company can sustain___ you comfortably for the rest of your life.
   the level of production already set.

3. ___An unusual person may commune___ with events in the future, so they say.

4. ___You may attain___ the position of manager.
   all the goals you have set.

5. ___You might denounce___ a friend for insulting you.
   the policies of a political party.

6. ___They revealed___ the secrets they were not to talk about.
   the identity of the mystery person.

7. ___The mixture will clot___ when its temperature is lowered.
   quickly when left in the sun.

8. ___She could be investigating___ an interesting research project.
   the reasons for the accident.

Notice the kinds of words that immediately follow the verb and the kinds of sentence models that fit with certain verbs. You will use these sentence patterns or models to help you write sentences in the next exercise.

Words in Use

On the lines below write sentences of your own using the correct form of the verb given in parentheses.

1. (attain) _____

_____

2. (commune) _____

_____

3. (conceive) _____

_____

4. (denounce) _____

_____

5. (reveal) _____

_____

6. (sustain) _____

_____

Exercise E
DEFINITIONS AND PARAPHRASES

After reading each of the incomplete phrases, select the correct word from the vocabulary list and write it in the blank to complete a paraphrase or definition. Correct choices show that you understand the meanings of the lesson words.

Words to Fill the Blanks

antithesis	conceive	nebulous
attain	denounce	reveal
census	divine	secular
clot	filament	spontaneous
commune	investigate	sustain

1. Events or persons that are (non-religious, not church-related, or _secular_)

2. To (think of, bring into being, imagine, or _conceive_) a new idea

3. (Holy, heavenly, sacred, or ___divine___) characters, who may be saints

4. To (arrive at, reach, gain, or ___attain___) a goal

5. To (blame, speak against, disapprove of, or ___denounce___) a person who commits a crime

6. A (poll, count, survey, or ___census___) of all males under 35 years of age

7. To (maintain, support, help, or ___sustain___) human life and health

8. To (be in touch with, contact, talk with, or ___commune___ with) other people

9. A (lump, mass, thickened part, or ___clot___) formed by heat or cold

10. A (line, thread, wire, or ___filament___) in an electrical connection

11. Honesty, the (opposite, reverse, contrast, or ___antithesis___) of dishonesty

12. To (show, disclose, expose, or ___reveal___) objects by shining a light on them

13. (An unplanned, a sudden, or a ___spontaneous___) laugh or cough

14. A (cloudy, unclear, vague, or ___nebulous___) explanation of a difficult topic

15. To (search, examine, look carefully at, or ___investigate___) evidence or data

LESSON

6

Vocabulary

agitate	console	elaborate
allude	contradict	heresy
anecdote	convene	hibernate
awe	deity	niche
collide	devastate	soluble

Exercise A

VOCABULARY IN CONTEXT

In the sentences below, the first sentence in each pair, sentence *a*, gives you enough context to make a decision about a general meaning for the study word in the sentence. After reading sentence *a*, decide whether sentence *b* is true or false. Mark your answer by putting an **X** in the *T* or *F* box before sentence *b*.

1. a. Unions often *agitate* employers by striking to get better working conditions for union members.

T ☒ F ☐   **b.** It would be reasonable to expect some emotional response from a friend you have *agitated*. *argued*

2. a. The governor *alludes* to the idea that he will run again for the governorship, although he has not stated his plan directly.

T ☒ F ☒   **b.** *Alluding* to ideas is the most direct way to present information. *to hint*

3. a. The old sailor told many *anecdotes* of his life sailing the oceans, but most of his stories were only half true.

T ☒ F ☐   **b.** Any normal adult has told and retold *anecdotes* about his or her life. *~ short stories*

4. a. Our feelings toward many famous people are feelings of *awe*—that is, feelings of respect and wonder.

T ☐ F ☒   **b.** Most ordinary people in a community are in *awe* of each other.

5. a. When two airplanes *collide* in the air, the accident is often the fault of one or both pilots. *hit/contact*

T ☒ F ☐   **b.** In order for objects to *collide* they must come into contact with one another.

51

6. a. Though his automobile was a total wreck, Tanaka was *consoled* by the fact that he was unhurt.   *comfort*

T ☐ F ☑ b. You might be expected to *console* a friend who has just won several thousand dollars.

7. a. The theory that the earth is flat was *contradicted* by sailors who sailed around the world.

T ☑ F ☐ b. If a story *contradicts* the facts, it is probably a lie.   *deny, oppose*

8. a. The Security Council of the United Nations *convenes* regularly and also whenever there is an international emergency.

T ☑ F ☐ b. We would expect the United States Senate to *convene* regularly.

9. a. Of all the gods of Greek mythology, the most powerful *deity* was Zeus, father of other gods.

T ☑ F ☐ b. In the belief of Christians, Jesus is a *deity*.   *God*

10. a. A typhoon can *devastate* an area, ruining property, destroying crops, and killing people.   *ruin, lay waste, destroy*

T ☑ F ☐ b. Certain events in people's lives can *devastate* them psychologically.

11. a. The royal wedding was the most *elaborate* ceremony England has seen in this century. Everything was planned to the smallest detail.   *detail, complicated*

T ☑ F ☑ b. The phrases "more *elaborate*" and "less simple" are similar in meaning.

12. a. A religious group member may be guilty of *heresy* if he holds a belief that his group considers false or in violation of its principles.

T ☑ F ☐ b. *Heresy* has probably led to new ideas and inventions.

13. a. Bears *hibernate* in winter, sleeping in their caves until spring, when they return to their normal daily activities.   *spend winter in a dormant state*

T ☑ F ☐ b. One would expect bodily functions of *hibernating* animals to slow down.

14. a. The bodies of the natives were placed in *niches* carved into the stone walls of the cave.   *a recess or hollow in a wall*

T ☑ F ☐ b. You would not expect to find a completely flat wall where there are *niches*.

15. a. Salt and sugar are *soluble* in water; that is, they combine with the water to form a solution.   *can be dissolved, become part of solution*

T ☑ F ☐ b. Sweetened coffee is a sign that sugar is *soluble*.

Exercise B

ANALOGIES

Choose a word from the list on the right to complete each analogy. Write the word you have chosen in the blank provided. You will *not* use three of the 18 words in the list.

1. **Hide** is to **show** as **contradict** is to ___agree with___   ✓touch

2. **Heat** is to **coolness** as **agitate** is to ___calmness___   delay

3. **Letter** is to **write** as **anecdote** is to ___tell___   ✓mixture

4. **Correct** is to **mistake** as **console** is to ___sadness___   —disagreement

5. **Sicken** is to **disease** as **devastate** is to ___earthquake___   ✓mind

6. **Ugly** is to **beautiful** as **elaborate** is to ___simple___   ✓senate

7. **Queen** is to **Elizabeth** as **deity** is to ___Buddha (praise)___   invention

8. **Table** is to **furniture** as **heresy** is to ___disagreement___   ✓simple

9. **Stool** is to **seat** as **niche** is to ___hole___   ✓agree with

10. **Laugh** is to **smile** as **collide** is to ___touch___   ✓hole

11. **Agreeable** is to **contract** as **soluble** is to ___rapture___   ✓calmness

12. **Dream** is to **imagine** as **hibernate** is to ___sleep___   ✓suggestion

13. **Sell** is to **sale** as **allude** is to ___suggestion___   ✓Buddha

14. **Hunger** is to **body** as **awe** is to ___mind___   trial

15. **Play** is to **orchestra** as **convene** is to ___senate___   ✓tell

✓sadness

✓earthquake

✓sleep

Exercise C
WORD FORMS: DERIVATIONS

Complete the following table by writing in the correct forms of the words already given in the table. Suffixes have been provided for you. The broken underline before each suffix indicates the number of letters you need to spell the correct, complete derivation. Be sure to put a letter over each dash. Derivative forms that do not change from the base forms, and those that have unusual spellings, are written out for you over the dashes.

Noun Form	Verb Form	Adjective Form	Adverb Form
1. agitation agitator	agitate		
2. allusion	allude		
3. awe	awe	awesome awful	awfully
4. collision	collide		

Noun Form	Verb Form	Adjective Form	Adverb Form
5. _consol_ation	console	_consol_atory	
6. _contradict_ion	contradict	_contradict_ory	
7. _conven_tion	convene	_conven_tional	_conventional_ly
8. _devastat_ion	devastate		
9. _elabora_tion	_e l a b o r a t e_	elaborate	_elaborate_ly
10. heresy			
_here_tic		_heretic_al	
11. _hibernat_ion	hibernate		
12. _solub_ility		soluble	
Solubility		in_soluble_	

Use words from this table to fill the blanks in the next exercise.

Sentence Completion

Use the table of derivative forms you have completed to fill the blanks in the following exercise. Use the noun, verb, adjective, or adverb form, depending upon the meaning of the sentence. The sentence numbers correspond to the numbers of the word groups in the table.

1. When the strike was in full progress, the ___*agitators*___ raised their signs and shouted loudly.

2. Poets use the process of ___*allusion*___ to create mental pictures by simple suggestion rather than by direct statement.

3. We are reminded of our ___*awe*___ of nature when we experience an earthquake or see the eruption of a volcano.

4. The earth is protected from severe ___*collision*___ with meteors and other heavenly bodies by its atmosphere, which causes these bodies to burn up before reaching the earth's surface.

5. A ___*consolating*___ attitude of one person toward another may indicate feelings of sympathy.

6. Progress in science may be made when researchers find ___*Contradictions*___ to existing theories.

7. A ___*convention*___ may bring together people who have similar interests or tastes, or who wish to solve a common problem.

8. Much of the ___*devastation*___ caused by fires could be prevented through the use of better warning or control systems.

9. A good storyteller can ___*elaborate*___ on a simple story by adding many descriptive details.

10. Martin Luther was considered a ___*heretic*___ by his church because he did not accept some of its basic beliefs.

11. The process of ___*hibernation*___ among animals has provided interesting data for researchers, who find that some animals are near death in this condition.

12. A substance that will *not* dissolve in a liquid such as water may be considered _____ ___*insoluble*___ .

Exercise D

WORD ASSOCIATIONS: COLLOCATIONS

Choose subject-verb patterns from the list to make complete, grammatical, and meaningful sentences. Write a *complete subject-verb pattern* in each blank. Each subject-verb pattern should be used in one of the blanks.

Subject-Verb Patterns

The union agitated   Dean Jones convened
The son alluded   A storm can devastate
The vehicle collided   The student elaborated
A nurse consoled   Some organisms hibernate
His story contradicted

1. ___*His story contradicted*___   a statement made previously.
                                      all possible and logical explanations.

2. ___*Dean Jones convened*___   a meeting of students and faculty.
                                  with other members of the committee.

3. _a nurse consoled_ the mother who lost her child.
the suffering patient.

4. _The union agitated_ (incited) against the poor working conditions.
the workers to strike.

5. _A storm can devastate_ the property in the city.
the psychological health of people.

6. _The son alluded to_ to the possibility of quitting his job.
to the idea of getting married.

7. _The student elaborated_ on his career plans more fully.
upon the outline of the paper.

8. _Some organisms hibernate_ for many years before becoming active.
only in extreme cold conditions.

9. _The vehicle collided_ with another car.
with another one in space.

Notice the kinds of words that immediately follow the verb and the kinds of sentence models that fit with certain verbs. You will use these sentence patterns or models to help you write sentences in the next exercise.

Words in Use

Write sentences of your own using the correct form of the verb given in parentheses.

1. (agitate) _____

_____

2. (allude) _____

_____

3. (collide) _____

_____

4. (console) _____

_____

5. (contradict) _____

_____

6. (convene) _____

_____

7. (devastate) _____

_____

Exercise E

DEFINITIONS AND PARAPHRASES

Select a word or word group from the vocabulary list and write it in the blank to complete a paraphrase or definition. Correct choices will show that you understand the meanings of the words of the lesson.

Words to Fill the Blanks

agitate ✓	console ✓	elaborate ✓
allude to ✓	contradict ✓	heresy ✓
anecdote	convene ✓	hibernation ✓
awe of ✓	deity ✓	niche ✓
collide with ✓	devastate ✓	soluble ✓

1. (A complex, a detailed, a complicated, or an _elaborate_) plan of action

2. (A _soluble_) substance, which can be dissolved, broken down, or disintegrated in most liquids

3. (Fear of, wonder about, respect for, or _awe of_) the power of nature

4. To (destroy, ruin, wreck, or _devastate_) an entire city

5. A (god, religious figure, saint, or _deity_) recognized by members of a religious group

6. To (sympathize with, calm, comfort, or _console_) a sad person

7. To (oppose, deny, argue against, or _contradict_) an earlier theory in science

8. The (period of inactivity, long sleep, or _hibernation_) of some animals in the cold season

9. To (hint at, imply, suggest, or _allude to_) an idea that is not said openly

10. The act of (_heresy_), which might be a statement of disbelief of, rejection of, or opposition to an established set of beliefs

11. (A tale, an account, a story, an _anecdote_ _prefer_) of a person's experience

12. A (hole, dugout, hollow place, or _niche_) in a wall

13. To (bump, hit, strike, or _collide with_) another automobile while you are driving

14. To (meet, gather, assemble, or _convene_) to discuss a problem

15. To (disturb, stir up, arouse, or _agitate_) people's feelings enough to cause anger

LESSON 7

Vocabulary

acquire	collapse	delinquent
administer	confirm	device
aggression	constitute	diplomat
category	contagious	execute
cell	convert	subordinate

Exercise A

VOCABULARY IN CONTEXT

In the sentences below, the first sentence in each pair, sentence *a*, gives you enough context to decide about a general meaning for the study word in the sentence. After reading sentence *a*, decide whether sentence *b* is true or false. Mark your answer by putting an **X** in the *T* or *F* box before sentence *b*.

1. a. One generally *acquires* a job more easily than one *acquires* happiness. *gets*

Vague T ☑ *best* F ☑   **b.** The color of your eyes and hair is *acquired* from your parents.

2. a. As chief executive, the President *administers* the laws made by Congress. *this*

T ☐   F ☑   **b.** Parents *administer* their children. *manage, govern*

3. a. The extreme form of *aggression* is war, but we find *aggression* in the everyday lives of people who seem not to care about hurting others, both physically and psychologically.

T ☑   F ☐   **b.** A hungry lion is apt to be *aggressive*. *combative, assaultive*

4. a. Two *categories* of study in the field of biology are botany and zoology.

T ☑   F ☐   **b.** "Male" and "female" are also *categories*. *classifications, groups*

5. a. The *cell* is the basic unit, whether we are talking about units of living matter or the rooms in a prison.

T ☑   F ☐   **b.** The living *cells* of a child's body multiply as the child grows into an adult.

6. a. The *collapse* of even the strongest buildings can be expected during an earthquake that measures at the top of the scale. *falling down, topple*

T ☑   F ☐   **b.** Political systems as well as buildings can *collapse*.

59

7. a. In order for a jury to find people guilty of crimes, their guilt must be *confirmed* by evidence.

T ☑ F ☐   b. An airline reservation that has been *confirmed* usually allows a passenger to be sure of a seat on the plane. *verified*

8. a. Two groups, the Senate and the House of Representatives, *constitute* the U.S. Congress; however, many lawmaking bodies around the world consist of only a single group. *make up, composed of*

T ☑ F ☐   b. Hydrogen and oxygen *constitute* water.

9. a. Some diseases are so *contagious* that travelers can pass them from country to country in a very short time. *be passed among people*

T ☑ F ☐   b. Laughter can be *contagious*.

10. a. The tourist who *converts* his money from *yen* to dollars, for example, must accept the exchange rate being offered on that day.

T ☑ F ☐   b. A Christian can be *converted* to Buddhism. *changed*

11. a. Persons between 13 and 19 years of age commit a large proportion of the crimes in the community. These *delinquent* teenagers account for more than 40 percent of all crimes. *derelict, remiss*

T ☐ F ☑   b. A *delinquent* bill payer has probably paid her bill on time.

12. a. A simple *device* for measuring heat and cold is the mercury thermometer; a more complex *device* for measuring heat is one read through a computer.

T ☐ F ☑   b. A *device* cannot be an instrument powered by electricity. *apparatus*

13. a. *Diplomats* such as ambassadors and representatives to the United Nations are chosen carefully by their governments. *ambassador, rep, minister*

T ☑ F ☐   b. The advice to "be *diplomatic*" means to choose your language and actions cautiously. *tactful*

14. a. Employers expect their workers to *execute* orders promptly and correctly.

T ☑ F ☐   b. The opposite of *executing* an order is ignoring it. *carry out*

15. a. The power of the human mind allows men and women to *subordinate* their ordinary animal drives to drives that make them social beings.

T ☐ F ☑   b. "Best" is *subordinate* to "least." *put secondary position inferior rank*

Exercise B

ANALOGIES

Choose a word from the list on the right to complete each analogy. Write the word you have chosen in the blank provided. You will *not* use three of the 18 words in the list.

1. **Operation** is to **operator** as **aggression** is to _____*aggressor*_____   spreading

2. **Dirty** is to **wash** as **delinquent** is to _____*arrest*_____   rise

3. **Remember** is to **forget** as **acquire** is to _____*lose*_____   shovel

4. **Easy** is to **simple** as **convert** is to _____*change*_____   positive

5. **School** is to **college** as **device** is to _shovel_   ✓completed

6. **Cooking** is to **chef** as **administering** is to _manage_   _challenge

7. **Bacteria** is to **germs** as **category** is to _division_   ✓slaves

8. **Delicious** is to **pleasing** as **contagious** is to _spready_   ✓manager

9. **Train** is to **animals** as **subordinate** is to _slaves_   ✓aggressor

10. **Spell** is to **alphabet** as **constitute** is to _elements_   ✓typhoon

11. **Carpenter** is to **builder** as **diplomat** is to _representative_   ✓elements

12. **Death** is to **poison** as **collapse** is to _typhoon_   ✓single

13. **Ask** is to **uncertain** as **confirm** is to _positive_   _decrease

14. **Twins** are to **double** as **cell** is to _single_   ✓representative

15. **Study** is to **learned** as **execute** is to _completed_   ✓division

✓change

✓arrest

✓lose

Exercise C

WORD FORMS: DERIVATIONS

Complete the following table by writing the correct form of the words in the table. Suffixes have been provided for you. The broken underline before each suffix indicates the number of letters you need to spell the correct, complete derivation. Be sure to put a letter over each dash. Derivative forms that do not change from the base forms, and those that have unusual spellings, are written out for you over the dashes.

Noun Form	Verb Form	Adjective Form	Adverb Form
1. a c q u i s i t i o n	acquire		
2. administration	administer	administrative	
administrator			
3. aggression			
aggressiveness		aggressive	aggressively
aggressor			

Noun Form	Verb Form	Adjective Form	Adverb Form
4. category	_categor_ize		
5. cell		_cell_ular	
6. collapse	_collapse_		
7. _confirm_ation	confirm		
8. _constitu_ent	constitute		
_constitut_ion		_constitution_al	
9. _contag_ion		contagious	
10. _conver_sion	convert		
convert			
11. _delinquen_cy		delinquent	
delinquent			
12. device	_devise_		
13. _execut_ion	execute		
_execut_ive			
_execut_ioner			
14. _subordinat_ion	subordinate	_subordinate_	

Use words from this table to fill the blanks in the next exercise.

Sentence Completion

Use the table of derivative forms you have completed to fill the blanks in this exercise. Use the noun, verb, adjective, or adverb form, depending upon the meaning of the sentence. The sentence numbers correspond to the numbers of the word groups in the table.

1. Biologists continue to study the factors that determine the ___*acquisition*___ of mental and physical characteristics in humans.

2. A vice-president is considered an assistant to the president, who is the chief ___*administrative*___ _____.

3. While a lion may be quite ___*aggressive*___ when it is hungry, it is ordinarily a peaceful animal.

4. Though a whale is ___*categorized*___ as a mammal, many people think of it as belonging to the fish family.

5. Some ___*cells*___ multiply at a very fast rate; yeast is a good example.

6. In spite of its greatness, the Roman Empire ___*collapsed*___ in the fifth century.

7. Before the pilot of a commercial jetliner can take off from the air field, he must wait for ___*confirmation*___ from the officials in the tower.

8. A ___*constitution*___ is a set of laws that regulate all the activities and procedures of a country or organization.

9. Many of the most highly ___*contagious*___ illnesses have been controlled through research and public health measures.

10. The ___*conversion*___ of water to steam creates the energy to run some of the world's heaviest machinery.

11. Statistics show that ___*delinquency*___, particularly crimes against other people, increases when unemployment rises.

12. Space scientists believe that it is possible to ___*devise*___ a space shelter large enough to house the population of a small city as it floats high above the earth.

13. An ___*executive*___ like the president of a company is generally one of the highest paid workers in the company.

14. Being successful in getting a university education requires one's ___*subordination*___ of immediate goals to long-range goals.

Exercise D

WORD ASSOCIATION: COLLOCATION

Choose subject-verb patterns from the list to make complete, grammatical, and meaningful sentences. Write a *complete subject-verb pattern* in the blank before each word group. Each subject-verb pattern should be used in one of the blanks.

Subject-Verb Patterns

You may acquire   The group constituted
The lawyer administered The traveler converted
We can categorize   The manager devised
The bridge collapsed   The employee executed
He confirmed   One group subordinated

1. *One group subordinated* another group by making slaves of the people. its goals to the goals of the majority.

2. *He confirmed* that he would take flight number 78. his willingness to accept the position.

3. *The group constituted* a majority of the voters in the country. only a part of the club membership.

4. *You may acquire* many negative habits without training. great wealth from oil deposits.

5. *The lawyer administered* the affairs of the company for many years. the association as its president.

6. *We can categorize* people by their height and weight.

7. *The bridge collapsed* with a loud roar and much dust.

8. *The traveler converted* all the foreign currency to dollars.

9. *The manager devised* a new plan for earning money for the company.

10. *The employee executed* the orders without a single complaint.

Notice the kinds of words that immediately follow the verb and the kinds of sentence models that fit with certain verbs. You will use these sentence patterns or models to help you write sentences in the next exercise.

Words in Use

Write sentences of your own using the correct form of the verb in parentheses.

1. (acquire)_____

_____

2. (administer) _____

_____

3. (collapse) _____

_____

4. (confirm) _____

_____

5. (constitute) _____

_____

6. (convert) _____

_____

7. (devise) _____

_____

8. (subordinate) _____

_____

Exercise E

DEFINITIONS AND PARAPHRASES

After reading each of the incomplete phrases, select a word from the vocabulary list and write it in the blank to complete a paraphrase or definition. Correct choices show that you understand the meanings of the lesson words.

Words to Fill the Blanks

acquire	collapse	delinquent
administer	confirm	devices
aggression	constitute	diplomat
category	contagious	execute
cell	convert	subordinate

1. A (____Contagious____) disease, one that is easily communicated, spread, or passed

   on to another person

2. A (____delinquent____) person, who fails to pay bills, breaks laws, or violates rules

3. A (____cell____), which may be a small unit of living matter, a small room,

   or a container

4. To (lower, put down, lessen the rank of, or ___*subordinate*___) a person or position

5. To (develop, get, gain, or ___*acquire*___) good habits through training

6. To (govern, take care of, manage, or ___*administer*___) a company or country

7. To (agree with, show the truth of, support, or ___*confirm with*___) an earlier theory through research

8. To (change, adapt, exchange, or ___*convert*___) old customs to new ones

9. To (perform, carry out, complete, or ___*execute*___) a duty or responsibility

10. To (make up, comprise, consist of, or ___*constitute*___), as the ingredients in any mixture

11. (Equipment, tools, instruments, or ___*devices*___) for laboratory research

12. A (representative, government official, or ___*diplomat*___) who takes care of the affairs of his or her government in another country

13. (An offensive, an attack, a war, or ___*aggression*___) against a neighboring country

14. The (fall, failure, break up, or ___*collapse*___) of a great empire

15. A (class, division, group, or ___*category*___) in a library collection

LESSON 8

Vocabulary

accelerate	conflict	pragmatic
adapt	consent	repress
assemble	decline	restore
circumstance	elated	rhythm
conduct	inert	spectrum

Exercise A

VOCABULARY IN CONTEXT

In the following sentences, the first sentence in each pair, sentence *a*, gives you enough context to make a decision about a general meaning for the lesson word in the sentence. After reading sentence *a*, decide whether sentence *b* is true or false. Mark your answer by putting an **X** in the *T* or *F* box before sentence *b*.

1. a. An object falling freely to earth will *accelerate* faster and faster until it reaches a maximum speed in its fall. *increase in speed; go faster*

    T ☒ F ☐ b. A ball rolling freely down a hill would illustrate the process of *acceleration*.

2. a. The cockroach is said to be a perfect example of the process of evolution. It has been able to *adapt* itself to almost any condition in the environment and thereby to outlive many other species. *change, modify*

    T ☐ F ☒ b. *Adapting* one's self to a situation is a physical adjustment, not a psychological one. *It's both sometimes.*

3. a. Congress *assembles* every year in Washington to consider new laws and changes in old laws. *meet*

    T ☒ F ☐ b. Meetings are held in an *assembly* hall.

4. a. A witness to a crime, an accident, or suspicious behavior should report such *circumstance* to the police. *occurence; fact or event accompanying another*

    T ☒ F ☐ b. It is possible that one *circumstance* may lead to another.

5. a. On a typical tour the guide *conducts* a group of 40 tourists on a ten-day trip among all of the Hawaiian Islands. *to lead; a leading guidance*

    T ☐ F ☒ b. Most teachers expect the students to *conduct* the class sessions.

67

6. a. A *conflict* of philosophies sometimes becomes a *conflict* of armies, as we have seen in many past wars. *fight, struggle, clash, opposition*

T ☑ F ☑   b. A wrestling match is a kind of *conflict*.

7. a. As a part of the marriage ceremony each partner must *consent* to the marriage by saying "I do." *concur, give permission, approval*

T ☑ F ☐   b. Someone who has given her *consent* has given her permission.

8. a. The use of oil lamps *declined* rapidly after electric power became widespread and cheap. *to lessen in force, value (downward slope) deteriorate, decay (vs)*

T ☐ F ☑   b. Your *declining* years are the years when you are young.

9. a. You would be *elated* to win a large sum of money, but unhappy on the other hand to learn how much tax must be paid on the money. *happy, excited*

T ☐ F ☑   b. People would normally be *elated* in preparing for their own funerals.

10. a. If the label on a product says "*inert* ingredients 96 percent," only 4 percent of the contents are doing the work for you; the rest may be plain water.

T ☑ F ☐   b. *Inertia* is a noun that means lack of activity. *inactive*

11. a. The typical *pragmatic* person believes that the value of a thought or theory is measured by its usefulness in everyday living. *practical (guided in business rules)*

T ☐ F ☑   b. All philosophers from ancient to modern times fit the *pragmatic* description.

12. a. Psychologists say that mental illness can be caused when people *repress* their feelings rather than show their feelings openly. *holding back, restrain, keep down*

T ☑ F ☐   b. The opposite of expressing a feeling is *repressing* a feeling.

13. a. It takes an expert to *restore* an old work of art to its original condition and beauty. *(representation of the original form)*

T ☑ F ☐   b. *Restoring* implies redoing. *time, temps, meter, flow, movement*

14. a. We see people tapping their feet in time with the *rhythm* of certain types of music, especially marching songs.

T ☑ F ☐   b. *Rhythm* has to do with regularity and timing.

15. a. The rainbow has the whole *spectrum* of colors. *range*

T ☑ F ☐   b. The color blue is a part of the *spectrum* of colors.

(series of colored bands diffracted & arranged in the order of their respective wave lengths)

Exercise B

ANALOGIES

Choose a word from the list on the right to complete the analogy. Write the word you have chosen in the blank provided. You will *not* use three of the 18 words in the list.

1. **Increase** is to **quantity** as **accelerate** is to ___*movement*___   active

2. **Cautious** is to **careless** as **inert** is to ___*active*___   open

3. **Depart** is to **leave** as **conduct** is to ___*lead*___   ✓ practical

4. **Divide** is to **separated** as **restore** is to ___*rebuilt*___   ✓ pleasure

5. Thoughtful is to decision as elated is to _pleasure_   ✓ deny

6. Gain is to increase as assemble is to _gather_   ✓ dance

7. Protected is to guarded as pragmatic is to _practical_   slow

8. Worry is to concern as circumstance is to _happen_   ✓ range

9. Sleep is to wake as consent is to _deny_   ✓ increase

10. Cure is to well as adapt is to _adjusted_   ✓ movement

11. Speed is to race as rhythm is to _dance_   ✓ rebuilt

12. Story is to tale as spectrum is to _range_   ✓ desires

13. Boredom is to interest as conflict is to _agreement_   ✓ agreement

14. Fail is to succeed as decline is to _increase_   ✓ adjusted

15. Imagine is to ideas as repress is to _desires_   bored

                                                       ✓ happening

                                                       ✓ gather

                                                       ✓ lead

Exercise C
WORD FORMS: DERIVATIONS

Complete the following table by writing in the correct forms of the words given in the table. Suffixes have been provided for you. The underline before each suffix indicates the number of letters you need to spell the correct, complete derivation. Be sure to put a letter over each dash. Derivative forms that do not change from the base forms, and those that have unusual spellings, are written out for you over the dashes.

Noun Form	Verb Form	Adjective Form	Adverb Form
1. accelerat ion accelerat or	accelerate		
2. adapt ability adapt ation	adapt	adapt ive	
3. assembl y	assemble		
4. circumstance		circumstan tial	

Noun Form	Verb Form	Adjective Form	Adverb Form
5. c o n d u c t _conduct_ or _conduct_ ivity _conduct_ ion	conduct		
6. conflict	c o n f l i c t		
7. c o n s e n t	consent		
8. d e c l i n e	decline		
9. _elat_ ion	e l a t e	elated	
10. _inert_ ia _inert_ ness		inert	
11. _pragmat_ ism		pragmatic	
12. _repress_ ion	repress		
13. _restor_ ation	restore		
14. rhythm		_rhythm_ ic	_rhythmic_ ally

Use words from this table to fill the blanks in the next exercise.

Sentence Completion

Use the table of derivative forms you have completed to fill the blanks in this exercise. Use the noun, verb, adjective, or adverb form, depending upon the meaning of the sentence. The sentence numbers correspond to the numbers of the word groups in the table.

1. Accidents are sometimes caused when the driver of a car presses the _____ _accelerator_ pedal instead of the brake.

2. The _adaptability_ of animals to a new environment is necessary for their survival in their new surroundings.

3. The soldiers ___assembled___ and prepared for the final attack.

4. Taxation without representation was one of the ___circumstances___ that led to the American Revolution.

5. Famous ___conductors___ of large symphony orchestras are often also great musicians.

6. The ___conflict___ between good and evil is a theme that has been used many times in stories all over the world.

7. Before a doctor can operate on an underage child, the parents must give their ___consent___.

8. A ___decline___ in the world supply of oil usually makes an increase in the price of gasoline.

9. High school graduates may be ___elated___ about completing their education but saddened about leaving their friends.

10. Powerful, quick-acting chemicals are often mixed with ___inert___ substances such as water to weaken them enough for proper use.

11. A truly ___pragmatic___ person would say that experience is the best teacher.

12. The ___repression___ of anger is often difficult, but we expect children to learn this type of control.

13. The ___restoration___ of great works of art requires much skill and patience, but keeping these art treasures in good condition is well worth the effort.

14. Drums are the major source of ___rhythm___ for a band as it marches.

Exercise D
WORD ASSOCIATIONS: COLLOCATIONS

Choose subject-verb patterns from the list to make complete, grammatical, and meaningful sentences. Write a *complete subject-verb pattern* in the blank before each word group. Each subject-verb pattern should be used in one of the blanks.

Subject-Verb Patterns

The car accelerated	The workers consented
Immigrants usually adapt	The country declined
The meeting assembled	It elated
The ideas conflicted	They are repressing
The guide conducted	Their hard work restored

1. _They are repressing_   their anger and hate.
   strong desires to quit school.

2. _The workers consented_   to give up their vacations this year.
   to a new contract with their employer.

3. _Their hard work restored_   the political party to power.
   the valuable painting to its original beauty.

4. _The meeting assembled_   in the large auditorium.
   at exactly 11 o'clock.

5. _The ideas conflicted_   with the opinions of the rest of the group.
   with the beliefs of the elders.

6. _The car accelerated_   as it rolled down the steep hill.

7. _The country declined_   rapidly after the terrible war.

8. _Immigrants usually adapt_   their customs to those of the new society.

9. _It elated_   him to find so many new friends.

10. _The guide conducted_   the tour through the mountains.

Notice the kinds of words that immediately follow the verb and the kinds of sentence models that fit with certain verbs. You will use these sentence patterns or models to help you write the sentences in the next exercise.

Words in Use

Write sentences of your own using the correct form of the verbs in parentheses.

1. (accelerate) _____

   _____

2. (adapt) _____

   _____

3. (assemble) _____

_____

4. (conflict) _____

_____

5. (consent) _____

_____

6. (decline) _____

_____

7. (repress) _____

_____

8. (restore) _____

_____

Exercise E

DEFINITIONS AND PARAPHRASES

After reading each of the incomplete phrases, select a word or word group from the vocabulary list to complete a paraphrase or definition. Correct choices show that you understand the meanings of the words of the lesson.

Words to Fill the Blanks

accelerate	conflict	pragmatic
adapt to	consent to	repress
assemble	decline	restore
circumstance	elated	rhythm
conduct	inert	spectrum

1. (An inactive, a passive, a nonactive, an ___*inert*___) part of a mixture

2. A (practical, realistic, ___*pragmatic*___) kind of person

3. (Happy, pleased, glad, ___*elated*___) because of good luck

4. (Agree to, permit, accept, ___*consent to*___) contract terms

5. The (beat, pattern, regularity, ___*rhythm*___) of the music

6. The (range, differences, scale, ___*spectrum*___) of bright to dark colors

7. To (decrease, fall apart, go down, _decline_) like a dying business

8. To (speed up, increase, quicken, _accelerate_) the forward movement

9. To (bring back, rebuild, put back, _restore_) the historic buildings

10. A (fight, struggle, disagreement, _conflict_) between two countries

11. To (fit into, adjust to, make oneself suitable to, _adapt to_) the customs of a society

12. (A happening, an event, a condition, a _circumstance_) that changes your life

13. To (gather, meet together, _assemble_) in a church or school

14. To (hold back, put down, control, _repress_) strong emotions

15. To (direct, lead, manage, _conduct_) a meeting or group

LESSON

9

Vocabulary

abandon	dimension	radical
atmosphere	dissolve	reinforce
charter	distinct	respond
consequence	proceed	seek
dictate	proposition	synthetic

Exercise A

VOCABULARY IN CONTEXT

In the sentences below, the first sentence in each pair, sentence *a*, gives you enough context to make a decision about a general meaning for the lesson word in the sentence. After reading sentence *a*, decide whether sentence *b* is true or false. Mark your answer by putting an **X** in the *T* or *F* box before sentence *b*.

1. a. When a volcano erupted on a Pacific island, the residents *abandoned* their homes and possessions and left the island by boat.

T ☐   F ☐   b. It would be wise to *abandon* a sinking ship.

2. a. It is believed that the gases from the world's industries are poisoning the *atmosphere*, so that one day the air surrounding the earth will not support life.

T ☐   F ☐   b. The *atmosphere* itself is made up of gases.

3. a. A *charter* is a kind of license or document written very much like a contract.

T ☐   F ☐   b. A bus or airplane *charter* would allow you to take your group on a special tour.

4. a. The most frequent *consequence* of too much food (or too many calories) is a fat body.

T ☐   F ☐   b. A *consequence* of gravity is that water will not run uphill.

5. a. A "buyer's market" means that the buyer may *dictate* the terms of the sale, sometimes including the price, to the seller.

T ☐   F ☐   b. A *dictator* can be a kind of commander.

75

6. a. One *dimension* of a box, or cube, is its width; the other *dimensions* are its height and length.

T ☐ F ☐   b. When we look at real objects, our eyesight allows us to see things in three *dimensions*.

7. a. A fixed amount of salt will *dissolve* in a certain amount of water. If there is too much salt in the water, however, it will settle to the bottom.

T ☐ F ☐   b. Plastic spoons *dissolve* easily in water.

8. a. A figure appeared at the window but the face was not *distinct* enough to be recognized.

T ☐ F ☐   b. The difference between the colors red and blue is not a *distinct* difference.

9. a. The Honolulu Marathon footrace *proceeds* from the middle of the island, around the southern end, and back again to the starting line.

T ☐ F ☐   b. A traffic sign that says "*Proceed* carefully" means that a driver should stop his automobile.

10. a. In bargaining situations the buyers make *propositions* that they expect the sellers to refuse; then the sellers make *propositions* that they expect the buyers to refuse. Eventually, the *propositions* that are accepted become the buying/selling price.

T ☐ F ☐   b. A *proposition* is similar to a proposal or an offer.

11. a. The most *radical* movement for change in a country is a revolution.

T ☐ F ☐   b. A very *radical* cure for a sore leg is to cut it off.

12. a. Doctors often give patients medicine by needle to *reinforce* the strength of the body to resist diseases.

T ☐ F ☐   b. Putting an extra lock on your front door is a kind of *reinforcement*.

13. a. A trained animal *responds* in some way to a simple signal or one-word command.

T ☐ F ☐   b. The pupil in the human eye *responds* to light and darkness.

14. a. Of all those who *seek* a career in the movies, only about 5 percent actually get to act in a picture.

T ☐ F ☐   b. There are probably more people who *seek* answers to questions than there are those who have found the right answers.

15. a. *Synthetic* fabrics—that is, manufactured or artificial materials—are the most widely used in the clothing industry today.

T ☐ F ☐   b. Sheep's wool is a *synthetic* material.

Exercise B

ANALOGIES

Choose a word from the list on the right to complete each analogy. Write the word you have chosen in the blank provided. You will *not* use three of the 18 words in the list.

1. Union is to marriage as proposition is to _____   stop

2. Bury is to cover as abandon is to _____   humans

3. Fight is to quarrel as charter is to _____ result

4. Quality is to honesty as dimension is to _____ unknown

5. Offer is to reward as dictate is to_____ solution

6. Scatter is to gather as reinforce is to_____ clear

7. Major is to minor as radical is to_____ length

8. Delicious is to good as distinct is to_____ moderate

9. Walk is to movement as respond is to_____ plastic

10. Style is to fashion as consequence is to _____ leave

11. Freeze is to liquid as dissolve is to_____ offer

12. Natural is to water as synthetic is to_____ go

13. Attack is to defend as proceed is to_____ weaken

14. Relieve is to painful as seek is to_____ strong

15. Water is to fish as atmosphere is to_____ orders

permit

behavior

lost

Exercise C
WORD FORMS: DERIVATIONS

Complete the table by writing in the correct forms of the words given in the table. The suffixes have been provided. Underlines before each suffix indicate the number of letters you need to spell the correct, complete derivation. Be sure to put a letter over each dash. Derivative forms that do not change from the base forms, and those that have unusual spellings, are written out for you over the dashes.

Noun Form	Verb Form	Adjective Form	Adverb Form
1. _ _ _ _ _ _ _ ment	abandon		
2. atmosphere		_ _ _ _ _ _ _ _ ic	
3. charter	c h a r t e r		
4. consequence		_ _ _ _ _ _ _ _ t	_ _ _ _ _ _ _ _ _ _ ly

Noun Form	Verb Form	Adjective Form	Adverb Form
5. _ _ _ _ _ _ ion	dictate		
_ _ _ _ _ _ or		_ _ _ _ _ _ orial	
_ _ _ _ _ _ orship			
6. dimension		_ _ _ _ _ _ _ _ _ al	
7. _ _ _ _ _ _ _ _ ion		distinct	_ _ _ _ _ _ _ _ ly
_ _ _ _ _ _ _ _ iveness		_ _ _ _ _ _ _ ive	_ _ _ _ _ _ _ _ _ _ _ ly
8. _ _ _ _ _ _ _ ings	proceed		
p r o c e d u r e			
9. r a d i c a l		radical	_ _ _ _ _ _ _ ly
10. _ _ _ _ _ _ _ _ _ ment	reinforce		
11. _ _ _ _ _ _ _ ent	respond		
r e s p o n s e		_ _ _ _ _ _ _ ive	
_ _ _ _ _ _ _ ibility		_ _ _ _ _ _ _ ible	
12.	_ _ _ _ _ _ size	synthetic	

Use words from this table to fill the blanks in the next exercise.

Sentence Completion

Use the table of derivative forms you have completed to fill the blanks in this exercise. Use the noun, verb, adjective, or adverb form, depending upon the meaning of the sentence. The sentence numbers correspond to the numbers of the word groups in the table.

1. It is illegal for parents to _____ their children because someone must

   take care of these dependents.

2. The _____ pressure of air is greater at sea level than it is at a height of 10,000 feet.

3. It would be reasonable to expect a _____ to be put into writing like a legal contract.

4. The taxes collected by a government are often less than the amount needed for running the government; _____, the budget must be cut.

5. A _____ husband or wife may cause problems that cannot be solved, except by divorce.

6. A picture in a book shows only two _____ to the human eye: length and width, but not depth.

7. The elephant is quite a _____ animal, with its great size and unusual trunk.

8. Good directions for learning how to do something should include careful, step-by-step _____ to follow.

9. Methods of transportation are _____ different from those used at the beginning of this century.

10. A vaccination for small pox is a means of _____ of the body's ability to resist that disease.

11. Most mothers feel a _____ for caring for their children's physical and psychological needs.

12. Laboratory scientists are now able to _____ vitamins exactly like those found in nature.

Exercise D
WORD ASSOCIATIONS: COLLOCATIONS

Choose subject-verb patterns from the list to make complete, grammatical, and meaningful sentences. Write a *complete subject-verb pattern* in each blank. Each subject-verb pattern should be used in one of the blanks.

Subject-Verb Patterns

The bear abandoned	Workers will reinforce
Let's charter	She responded
The king dictated	They can synthesize
He proceeded	

1. _____   the dam to hold back the river.
                          the old bridge until it is rebuilt.

2. _____   the terms of the marriage agreement.
                          orders to his troops to fight the enemy.

3. _____   her young ones in the cave.
                          the home used for the winter.

4. _____   several compounds using new techniques.
                          material that resembles real diamonds.

5. _____   to tell his story to the police officer.
                          down the road at a slow speed.

6. _____   to the question with the right answer.
                          to his insults with violent emotion.

7. _____   a bus to travel across the country.

Notice the kinds of words that immediately follow the verb and the kinds of sentence models that fit with certain verbs. You will use these sentence patterns or models to help you write sentences in the next exercise.

Words in Use

Write sentences of your own using the correct form of the verb in parentheses.

1. (abandon) _____

_____

2. (dictate) _____

_____

3. (proceed) _____

_____

4. (reinforce) _____

_____

5. (respond) _____

_____

6. (synthesize) _____

_____

Exercise E

DEFINITIONS AND PARAPHRASES

After reading each of the incomplete phrases, select a word or word group from the vocabulary list and write it in the blank to complete a paraphrase or definition. Correct choices show that you understand the meanings of the words of the lesson.

Words to Fill the Blanks

abandon	dimensions	radical
atmosphere	dissolve	reinforce
charter	distinct	respond to
consequence	proceed	seek
dictate	proposition	synthetic

1. (A revolutionary, an extreme, a complete, or a _____) change in thinking

2. (A clear, an easily seen, an easily understood, or a _____) difference in beliefs

3. (A manufactured, a human-made, a laboratory-made, or a _____) type of material

4. The (layer of gases, air, surrounding climate, or _____) of the earth

5. A (license, contract, document, or _____) that forms an agreement

6. To (command, order, direct, or _____) that the workers carry out a certain job

7. To (react to, reply to, answer, or _____) someone's question

8. To (break up, disappear, enter a solution, or _____) like salt in water

9. To (support, strengthen, build up, or _____) a weak structure

10. The (measurements, extent, size, or _____) of a piece of land

11. (A plan, an offer, a deal, or a _____) between buyer and seller

12. The (effect, result, outcome, or _____) of an accident

13. To (advance, continue, go ahead, or _____) from one point to another

14. To (search for, look for, try to find, or _____) a solution to a problem

15. To (give up, quit, leave, or _____) a project that is boring

LESSON 10

Vocabulary

accurate	intuition	strata
clergy	microbe	successor
cohesion	phase	testify
criterion	rural	trace
domestic	skeleton	treaty

Exercise A

VOCABULARY IN CONTEXT

In the sentences below, the first sentence in each pair, sentence *a*, gives you enough context to make a decision about a general meaning for the lesson word in the sentence. After reading sentence *a*, decide whether sentence *b* is true or false. Mark your answer by putting an X in the *T* or *F* box before sentence *b*.

1. **a.** In order to make an *accurate* judgment as to the winner of a horse race, a photograph is taken as the horses cross the finish line.

   T ☐ F ☐ **b.** Psychology is considered a more *accurate* science than physics.

2. **a.** Members of the *clergy* have various special titles like priest, minister, or monk.

   T ☐ F ☐ **b.** Most electricians and carpenters belong to the *clergy*.

3. **a.** *Cohesion* is the process or condition of sticking or holding together. It is *cohesion*, for example, that holds the molecules of water together.

   T ☐ F ☐ **b.** Culture is a force that works for *cohesion* in a group of people.

4. **a.** The age *criterion* for voting in many countries is 21. Other *criteria* might be citizenship in a country and residency in a certain area.

   T ☐ F ☐ **b.** Passing a driving test is a *criterion* for getting a driver's license.

5. **a.** *Domestic* animals such as cats and dogs have wild ancestors like the tiger and wolf.

   T ☐ F ☐ **b.** A synonym for *domestic* is *tame*.

83

6. **a.** *Intuition* is the power to know something without thinking about it and using logic or reason. Some people appear to have more of this power than others have.

T ☐ F ☐   **b.** In addition to our other five senses, we might call *intuition* our "sixth sense."

7. **a.** *Microbes*, such as bacteria, are such small organisms that we need a microscope to see them.

T ☐ F ☐   **b.** *Microbes* are often associated with diseases.

8. **a.** The first *phase* of building a large hotel is laying a strong foundation. The final *phase* of the work comes many months later.

T ☐ F ☐   **b.** When you use the word *phase*, you are talking about one step in a sequence.

9. **a.** In most countries the *rural* areas, or farming areas, have fewer problems of population overcrowding than the cities have.

T ☐ F ☐   **b.** Most of the land of Russia might be considered *rural*.

10. **a.** The *skeleton* provides the body with a structure of bones for support and protection.

T ☐ F ☐   **b.** A *skeleton* plan is probably something like an outline.

11. **a.** The *strata* or layers of air space that surround the earth have various titles, but for humans the most important layer is the atmosphere.

T ☐ F ☐   **b.** We could refer to the middle class as one of the *strata* of society.

12. **a.** A newly elected president is the *successor* to the old one.

T ☐ F ☐   **b.** A *successor* to a king's throne might be his daughter or son.

13. **a.** Witnesses who *testify* in a courtroom must swear to tell the truth when they speak for or against the person being tried.

T ☐ F ☐   **b.** Famous people who are pictured in advertisements for products appear to be *testifying* that the products are good.

14. **a.** Persons reported as missing often disappear so completely that not even a *trace* of them can be found.

T ☐ F ☐   **b.** If a substance contains a *trace* of copper, we can expect that the substance is not mainly copper.

15. **a.** A *treaty* is an agreement, usually between or among countries—like the Treaty of Versailles, which ended World War I, or the North Atlantic Treaty, which joins countries together in defense.

T ☐ F ☐   **b.** A *treaty* seems to be a kind of contract.

Exercise B

ANALOGIES

Choose a word from the list on the right to complete the analogy. Write the word you have chosen in the blank provided. You will *not* use three of the 18 words in the list.

1. **Photographs** are to **pictures** as **strata** are to _____   mind

2. **Tropical** is to **jungle** as **rural** is to _____   agreement

3. **Broad** is to **narrow** as **domestic** is to _____   man

4. **Study** is to **school** as **testify** is to _____   farm

5. **Movement** is to **body** as **intuition** is to _____   correctness

6. **Actor** is to **performer** as **microbe** is to _____   wild

7. **Production** is to **development** as **cohesion** is to _____   next

8. **Good** is to **quality** as **trace** is to _____   religion

9. **Hard** is to **firmness** as **accurate** is to _____   tame

10. **Chapter** is to **book** as **phase** is to _____   standard

11. **Law** is to **rule** as **criterion** is to _____   attraction

12. **Pupil** is to **student** as **treaty** is to _____   bone

13. **Family** is to **sister** as **skeleton** is to _____   quantity

14. **Ancestor** is to **before** as **successor** is to _____   sequence

15. **Doctor** is to **medicine** as **clergy** is to _____   disease

                                                        organism

                                                        court

                                                        levels

Exercise C
WORD FORMS: DERIVATIONS

Complete the following table by writing in the correct forms of the words given in the table. The suffixes have been provided, and the underline before each suffix indicates the number of letters you need to spell the correct, complete derivation. Be sure to put a letter over each dash. Derivative forms that do not change from the base forms, and those that have unusual spellings, are written out over the dashes.

Noun Form	Verb Form	Adjective Form	Adverb Form
1. _ _ _ _ _ _ cy		accurate	_ _ _ _ _ _ _ _ ly
2. cohesion		_ _ _ _ _ ive	_ _ _ _ _ _ _ _ ly
3.	_ _ _ _ _ _ _ _ ate	domestic	_ _ _ _ _ _ _ _ ally
4. intuition	i n t u i t	_ _ _ _ _ _ ive	_ _ _ _ _ _ _ _ _ ly

Noun Form	Verb Form	Adjective Form	Adverb Form
5. microbe		_ _ _ _ _ _ ial	
6. skeleton		_ _ _ _ _ _ al	
7. strata (pl.) stratum (sing.) _ _ _ _ _ ification	_ _ _ _ _ ify		
8. successor _ _ _ _ _ _ _ ion	s <u>u</u> c c <u>ee</u> d	_ _ _ _ _ _ _ ive	_ _ _ _ _ _ _ _ _ _ ly
9. _ _ _ _ _ mony	testify		
10. trace	t <u>r</u> a c <u>e</u>		

Use words from this table to fill the blanks in the next exercise.

Sentence Completion

Use the table of derivative forms you have completed to fill the blanks in this exercise. Use the noun, verb, adjective, or adverb form, depending upon the meaning of the sentence. The sentence numbers correspond to the numbers of the word groups in the table.

1. Scientists can _____ predict the movements of the moon and the ocean tides.

2. The society in general and the family in particular are strong _____ _____ forces in our lives.

3. Human beings advanced in their development as a species when they _____ _____ animals for work and food.

4. Animals appear to have an _____ sense of a coming earthquake long before the quake is felt by humans.

5. _____ forms, such as certain bacteria, can be controlled by penicillin.

6. Muscles that help the body move and control the bone structure are known as _____

_____ muscles.

7. The surface of the earth is formed in layers of various rock and soft material. These layers were formed through a process of _____.

8. A _____ of kings and queens over the centuries has kept the royal family on the throne of England.

9. The _____ of an eyewitness, someone who has seen a crime as it happened, is considered the best evidence in a courtroom trial.

10. Many human beings can _____ the history of their ancestors back for at least four generations.

Exercise D

WORD ASSOCIATION: COLLOCATION

Choose subject-verb patterns to make complete, grammatical, and meaningful sentences. Write a *complete subject-verb pattern* in the blank before each word group. Each subject-verb pattern should be used in one of the blanks.

Subject-Verb Patterns

We have domesticated	You may succeed
One might intuit	The actor testified
It is possible to stratify	Historians have traced

1. _____   against his friend during a court trial.
   for a commercial product being advertised.

2. _____   a society on the basis of wealth.
   people by their scores on a test.

3. _____   your father or mother as head of the family.
   the president of your club by election.

4. _____   ways to handle the affairs of life.
   the answer to a problem.

5. _____   wild elephants and horses.

6. _____   the growth of the Roman Empire.

Notice the kinds of words that immediately follow the verb and the kinds of sentence models that fit with certain verbs. You will use these sentence patterns or models to write sentences in the next exercise.

Words in Use
Write sentences of your own using the correct form of the verb in parentheses.

1. (domesticate) _____

   _____

2. (intuit) _____

   _____

3. (stratify) _____

   _____

4. (succeed) _____

   _____

5. (testify) _____

   _____

6. (trace) _____

   _____

Exercise E
DEFINITIONS AND PARAPHRASES

Select a word or word group from the vocabulary list and write it in the blank to complete a paraphrase or definition. Correct choices show that you understand the meanings of the lesson words.

Words to Fill the Blanks

accurate	intuition	strata
clergy	microbes	successor to
cohesion	phase	testify
criterion	rural	trace
domestic	skeleton	treaty

1. Animals that are (tame, not wild, or _____)

2. A (section, part of the sequence, stage, or _____) in your life

3. To (state, swear, declare, or _____) that you are honest

4. A report that is (without error, correct, true, or _____)

5. The (replacement for, next in line for, heir to, or _____) the title of head of the family

6. (A small quantity, a visible of sign, evidence, or a _____) of poison in the water

7. The (bony structure, support, framework, or _____) of an animal's body

8. (A noncity, an agricultural, or a _____) area of a country

9. (An agreement, a contract, a deal, or a _____) among nations

10. The (ministers, preachers, monks, or _____) of a church or temple

11. (Germs, bacteria, organisms, or _____) that are seen only with microscopes

12. The (layers, levels, or _____) of the earth's surface

13. (Insight, instinctive thinking, inborn sense, or _____) that helps us make quick, even automatic, decisions

14. A (model, standard, rule, or _____) by which we might judge the characters of others

15. The (joining, holding together, sticking together, or _____) of people of a single culture

LESSON

11

Vocabulary

attribute	external	sphere
conform	frustrate	stable
contend	grant	substantial
doctrine	incline	vacate
ethics	infect	velocity

Exercise A

VOCABULARY IN CONTEXT

In these sentences, the first sentence in each pair, sentence *a*, gives you enough context to make a decision about a general meaning for the vocabulary word in the sentence. After reading sentence *a*, decide whether sentence *b* is true or false. Mark your answer by putting an **X** in the *T* or *F* box before sentence *b*.

1. a. Among the *attributes* of democracy are four basic freedoms: freedom of speech and religion, freedom from want, and freedom from fear.

T ☐ F ☐ b. *Attribute* and *characteristic* have about the same meaning.

2. a. Members of a cultural group remain members of that group by *conforming* to its customs. Those who don't *conform* either leave or become outcasts.

T ☐ F ☐ b. Habits are examples of ways in which people *conform*.

3. a. In a political election each candidate *contends* that his or her ideas are the best.

T ☐ F ☐ b. You can *contend* that you are right even when you are wrong.

4. a. Each religion has its own set of *doctrines*, which it teaches its followers. These principles must be accepted by the group, in most cases.

T ☐ F ☐ b. In order for any principle to become a *doctrine* it must be written down.

5. a. Our *ethics*, the rules for right and wrong behavior, are formed by our culture.

T ☐ F ☐ b. Anyone who has no religion probably has not formed a set of *ethics*.

91

6. a. The skin of the body is a kind of *external* shell that has many functions besides protecting the internal organs.

T ☐ F ☐   b. Your nose is an *external* organ.

7. a. Many students are *frustrated* by the fact that they read so slowly it takes hours to read an assignment.

T ☐ F ☐   b. *Frustration* is related to disappointment.

8. a. Scholarships are *granted* regularly to good students in need of financial help.

T ☐ F ☐   b. Before a medical operation can be performed, it is customary for the patient or family to *grant* permission for the surgery.

9. a. There is an old theory that fat people are *inclined* to be jokers who laugh a lot.

T ☐ F ☐   b. Your personality is probably determined to a large extent by the emotions you are *inclined* toward.

10. a. Scientists discovered that people suffering from typhoid fever were *infected* by bacteria in their water supply.

T ☐ F ☐   b. A person with the flu has an *infection*.

11. a. The earth is nearly a *sphere*, but slightly egg-shaped, and about 25,000 miles around at the equator.

T ☐ F ☐   b. An American football is not a *sphere*.

12. a. Prices generally remain *stable* when supply and demand are balanced.

T ☐ F ☐   b. A good synonym for *stable* is *steady*.

13. a. There has been a *substantial* increase of nearly 40 percent in airplane fares in the last year, more than all the increases of the previous five years combined.

T ☐ F ☐   b. *Substantial* probably means more than "a little."

14. a. If you do not pay your rent, your landlord will ask you to *vacate* your apartment.

T ☐ F ☐   b. You might expect a room that has been *vacated* to be empty.

15. a. Sound travels through the air at a *velocity* of about 1100 feet per second.

T ☐ F ☐   b. Noise travels through the air at the *velocity* of sound.

Exercise B

ANALOGIES

Choose a word from the list on the right to complete the analogy. Write the word you have chosen in the blank provided. You will *not* use three of the 18 words in the list.

1. Feature is to appearance as attribute is to_____   inner

2. Create is to invent as conform is to_____   changeable

3. Solve is to problem as contend is to_____   afraid

4. Disease is to suffer as doctrine is to_____   amount

5. Plans are to **development** as ethics are to _____   believe

6. Common is to rare as external is to _____   character

7. Fear is to **danger** as frustrate is to_____   follow

8. Crush is to **smash** as grant is to_____   outside

9. **Employ** is to **hire** as incline is to_____   diameter

10. Battle is to **troops** as infect is to_____   leave

11. Cube is to **width** as sphere is to_____   argument

12. Ripe is to **immature** as stable is to_____   job

13. Near is to **distance** as substantial is to_____   behavior

14. Turn is to **twist** as vacate is to_____   virus

15. Degree is to **temperature** as velocity is to_____   problem

movement

give

lean toward

Exercise C

WORD FORMS: DERIVATIONS

Complete the following table by writing in the correct forms of the vocabulary words. Suffixes have been provided for you. The underline before each suffix indicates the number of letters you need to spell the correct, complete derivation. Be sure to put a letter over each dash. Derivative forms that do not change from the base forms, and those that have unusual spellings, are written out for you over the dashes.

Noun Form	Verb Form	Adjective Form	Adverb Form
1. attribute	a t t r i b u t e		
2. _ _ _ _ _ _ _ ity	conform		
3. c o n t e n t i o n	contend		
4. doctrine			
i n d o c t r i n a t i o n i n d o c t r i n a t e			

Noun Form	Verb Form	Adjective Form	Adverb Form
5. ethics		_ _ _ _ _ al	_ _ _ _ _ _ _ ly
6.		external	_ _ _ _ _ _ _ _ ly
7. _ _ _ _ _ _ _ _ ion	frustrate		
8. grant	g r a n t		
9. i n c l i n e	incline		
_ _ _ _ _ _ ation			
10. _ _ _ _ _ _ ion	infect	_ _ _ _ _ _ ious	
11. sphere			
_ _ _ _ _ icity		_ _ _ _ _ ical	
12. _ _ _ _ ility		stable	
_ _ _ _ ilization	_ _ _ _ ilize		
13.		substantial	_ _ _ _ _ _ _ _ _ _ _ ly
14.	vacate	v a c a n t	

Use words from this table to fill the blanks in the next exercise.

Sentence Completion

Use the table of derivative forms you have completed to fill the blanks in this exercise. Use the noun, verb, adjective, or adverb form, depending upon the meaning of the sentence. The sentence numbers correspond to the numbers of the word groups in the table.

1. We expect average human beings to have good and bad _____.

2. Societies or cultures are held together by the members' _____ to the

    beliefs of those societies or cultures.

3. It is quite natural to find _____ between two different political parties during an election period.

4. Parents attempt to _____ their children by teaching them ways to become good citizens.

5. Professional people, such as doctors or lawyers, must agree to follow certain _____ _____ rules in order to get a license to practice.

6. Medicines that can be used only _____ must not be taken by mouth.

7. Children who do not receive enough love and care from their parents may show the effects of _____.

8. Many governments _____ scholarships to good students whose fields of study are considered essential for their countries.

9. A majority of university students have an _____ to study, but a few are not willing to work hard.

10. One _____ disease known as the "black death," or bubonic plague, killed many people during the fourteenth century.

11. We know that the shape of the moon is _____; however, its surface is quite rough.

12. The _____ of a business depends upon its ability to make money—that is, profit.

13. Electronic computers have changed _____ over the years.

14. The school library is nearly _____ on Saturday evenings, but on Sunday afternoons it is again full of students.

Exercise D
WORD ASSOCIATION: COLLOCATION

Choose subject-verb patterns to make complete, grammatical, and meaningful sentences. Write a *complete subject-verb pattern* in the blank before each word group. Each subject-verb pattern should be used in one of the blanks.

Subject-Verb Patterns

We attribute	He is inclined
That idea conforms	They indoctrinated
She contends	They were infected
She was frustrated	The president stabilized
The committee granted	We will vacate

1. _____ the economy by increasing production.
   the failing company with a money loan.

2. _____ to be careless and unorganized.
   toward doing things in a hurry.

3. _____ in her efforts to achieve fame in acting.

4. _____ with the government regulations.
   with the evidence from other experiments.

5. _____ his mistake to his ignorance and youth.
   her personality to her happy life.

6. _____ that she was not late for work.
   that the new plan is the best one.

7. _____ scholarships to 40 new students.

8. _____ their followers with the new philosophy.

9. _____ with the disease germs from the water.

10. _____ the apartment before December of this year.

Notice the kinds of words that immediately follow the verb and the kinds of sentence models that fit with certain verbs. You will use these sentence patterns or models to write sentences in the next exercise.

Words in Use

Write sentences of your own using the correct form of the verb in parentheses.

1. (attribute) _____

   _____

2. (conform) _____

   _____

3. (contend) _____

_____

4. (grant) _____

_____

5. (indoctrinate) _____

_____

6. (infect) _____

_____

7. (stabilize) _____

_____

8. (vacate) _____

_____

Exercise E
DEFINITIONS AND PARAPHRASES

Select a word or word group from the vocabulary list to complete a paraphrase or defini-tion. Correct choices show that you understand the meanings of the words of the lesson.

Words to Fill the Blanks

attribute	external	sphere
conform with	frustrate	stable
contend	grant	substantial
doctrine	incline toward	vacate
ethics	infect	velocity

1. (An unchanging, a regular, a steady, or a _____) set of weather

conditions

2. To (argue, assert, maintain, or _____) that you are correct in your

decision

3. To (give, allow, permit, or _____) freedom of speech and religion

4. A (large, more than usual, heavy, or _____) sum of money

5. To (leave, move out of, empty, or _____) an old house to move to a new one

6. An (outer, outside, outward, or _____) layer like the skin on the body

7. A (globe, ball, round shape, or _____) similar to the shape of the earth

8. To (tend toward, lean toward, prefer, or _____) bright colored dresses or ties

9. (Rules, morals, behavior guides, or _____) by which we direct our lives

10. Problems that (worry, disappoint, discourage, or _____) human beings

11. To (obey, follow, agree with, or _____) the rules of the game

12. Organisms that (contaminate, poison, attack, or _____) the body

13. The (speed, rate of movement, acceleration, or _____) of a body falling through space

14. The (law, belief, principle, or _____) of "live and let live"

15. (A characteristic, a quality, a property, or an _____) of the human personality

LESSON 12

Vocabulary

acute	edit	launch
barbarian	exert	orbit
conserve	extract	perspective
dissociate	incident	scheme
dominate	intense	segment

Exercise A

VOCABULARY IN CONTEXT

In the sentences below, the first sentence in each pair, sentence *a*, gives you enough context to make a decision about a general meaning for the vocabulary word in the sentence. After reading sentence *a*, decide whether sentence *b* is true or false. Mark your answer by putting an **X** in the *T* or *F* box before sentence *b*.

1. a. A long period without rain in a farm area of a country can cause an *acute* shortage of food.

T ☐ F ☐   **b.** There are always plenty of jobs during an *acute* unemployment situation.

2. a. There are few, if any, *barbarians*—for example, members of uncivilized, savage tribes—left in the world today.

T ☐ F ☐   **b.** It is likely that *barbarian* people do not know how to read and write.

3. a. We can *conserve* energy by using less electricity and gasoline.

T ☐ F ☐   **b.** Reusing old metal is a means of *conserving* natural resources.

4. a. When a business partnership is broken, the partners legally *dissociate* themselves from one another.

T ☐ F ☐   **b.** A divorce between a husband and wife is a kind of *dissociation*.

5. a. Even today, the members of some cultures are *dominated* by a chief who has complete control of their affairs.

T ☐ F ☐   **b.** According to the laws of nature, the strong are able to *dominate* the weak.

99

6. a. On every big newspaper someone *edits* the writing of reporters to make sure that their reports are clear and correctly worded.

T ☐ F ☐   b. A book that has been *edited* has been changed in some way.

7. a. When you blow up a balloon, you can see the force *exerted* by air pressure on the inside of the container.

T ☐ F ☐   b. Gravity is a force *exerted* upon you every minute of your life.

8. a. The milky oil of the coconut is *extracted* by squeezing the meat, which has been removed from the shell.

T ☐ F ☐   b. Those who have had all their teeth *extracted* are toothless.

9. a. Although the accident happened at 5 P.M., the *incident* was not reported until two hours later.

T ☐ F ☐   b. The following report would be a good, or favorable, one: "The operation was performed without *incident*."

10. a. Because the noonday sun is the most *intense*, it causes the worst sunburn to those on the beach.

T ☐ F ☐   b. A person with *intense* feelings is likely to be emotional.

11. a. The campaign to wipe out smallpox was *launched* when scientists first used a weakened smallpox virus for injection or vaccination of human beings.

T ☐ F ☐   b. A war that is about to be *launched* by one country against another has not started as yet.

12. a. With each *orbit* around the earth our manufactured satellites give us back valuable weather data.

T ☐ F ☐   b. The earth makes a complete *orbit* around the sun in about 365¼ days.

13. a. A vacation helps one to get a new *perspective*, or a new way of looking at one's daily life and work.

T ☐ F ☐   b. A *perspective* might also be known as a "point of view."

14. a. There are probably many *schemes* for getting rich quickly, but only a few of these plans are likely to be successful.

T ☐ F ☐   b. Every project with a good *scheme* is going to be successful.

15. a. If the peel is taken off an orange, the fruit can be broken into *segments* and eaten easily.

T ☐ F ☐   b. A line drawn through a circle cuts it into two *segments*.

Exercise B

ANALOGIES

Choose a word from the list on the right to complete each analogy. Write the word you have chosen in the blank provided. You will *not* use three of the 18 words in the list on the right.

1. Sentence is to **paragraph** as **segment** is to_____   problem

2. Model is to **pattern** as **barbarian** is to_____   weak

3. Locate is to find as extract is to _____ save

4. Smell is to odor as incident is to _____ join

5. Enter is to exit as dissociate is to _____ designer

6. Float is to sink as conserve is to _____ pressure

7. Outline is to writer as scheme is to _____ whole

8. Graduate is to completion as launch is to _____ writing

9. Overdue is to bill as acute is to _____ round

10. Test is to examination as perspective is to _____ end

11. Repair is to machinery as edit is to _____ control

12. Heavy is to light as intense is to _____ savage

13. Request is to ask as dominate is to _____ part

14. Cube is to rectangular as orbit is to _____ waste

15. Feel is to emotion as exert is to _____ beginning

remove

viewpoint

event

Exercise C
WORD FORMS: DERIVATIONS

Complete the following table by writing in the correct forms of the words in the table. Suffixes have been provided. The underline before each suffix indicates the number of letters you need to spell the correct, complete derivation. Be sure to put a letter over each dash. Derivative forms that do not change from the base forms, and those that have unusual spellings, are written out for you over the dashes.

Noun Form	Verb Form	Adjective Form	Adverb Form
1. _ _ _ _ _ ness		acute	_ _ _ _ _ ly
2. barbarian		b a r b a r i a n	
_ _ _ _ _ _ ism		_ _ _ _ _ _ ous	_ _ _ _ _ _ _ _ _ ly
		_ _ _ _ _ _ ic	

Noun Form	Verb Form	Adjective Form	Adverb Form
3. _ _ _ _ _ _ _ ation	conserve	_ _ _ _ _ _ _ ative	_ _ _ _ _ _ _ _ _ _ _ _ ly
4. _ _ _ _ _ _ _ _ ion	dissociate		
5. _ _ _ _ _ _ _ ion _ _ _ _ _ ance d o m i n i o n	dominate	_ _ _ _ _ ant	
6. _ _ _ _ ion _ _ _ _ or _ _ _ _ orial	edit	_ _ _ _ orial	
7. _ _ _ _ _ ion	exert		
8. e x t r a c t _ _ _ _ _ _ or _ _ _ _ _ _ ion	extract	_ _ _ _ _ _ _ able	
9. incident _ _ _ _ _ ence		_ _ _ _ _ _ _ al	_ _ _ _ _ _ _ _ _ _ ly
10. _ _ _ _ _ _ ity	_ _ _ _ _ _ ify	intense _ _ _ _ _ _ ive	_ _ _ _ _ _ _ _ _ ly
11. orbit	o r b i t	_ _ _ _ _ al	
12. scheme	s c h e m e	_ _ _ _ _ atic	_ _ _ _ _ _ _ _ _ ally
13. segment	s e g m e n t	_ _ _ _ _ _ _ al	

Use words from this table to fill the blanks in the next exercise.

Sentence Completion

Use the table of derivative forms you have completed to fill the blanks in this exercise. Use the noun, verb, adjective, or adverb form, depending upon the meaning of the sentence. The sentence numbers correspond to the numbers of the word groups in the table.

1. The _____ of economic inflation in a country can be measured by the rise in the prices of goods over a period of time.

2. Eating human flesh is considered _____ in most cultures of the world.

3. A truly _____ person would probably be slow to make any major changes in life.

4. When parts of countries _____ from one another new, independent nations are born.

5. Albert Einstein was a _____ figure in science during his lifetime.

6. The _____ section of the daily newspaper is the place where opinions are expressed by the newspaper management.

7. In addition to the force of gravity, air pressure _____ a regular force upon the human body.

8. The _____ of oil from coconut meat is a regular daily process in the lives of many islanders.

9. Two persons who witness the same _____ may give quite different reports about what they have seen.

10. Newborn infants who are born before their full development in the womb are given _____ _____ care in their first few months.

11. The planets of the solar system stay in regular _____ paths around the sun.

12. A university education usually follows an educational _____ that leads to a degree in a particular field of study.

13. Making judgments about an entire society on the basis of the characteristics of a _____ _____ of that society may lead to incorrect conclusions.

Exercise D

WORD ASSOCIATIONS: COLLOCATIONS

Choose subject-verb patterns to make complete, grammatical, and meaningful sentences. Write a *complete subject-verb pattern* in the blank before each word group. Each subject-verb pattern should be used in one of the blanks.

Subject-Verb Patterns

The people conserved	The police intensified
She dissociated	The politicians launched
The man dominates	It orbitted
He edits	They schemed
It exerts	Disagreement can segment
A specialist can extract	

1. _____ useful minerals from the earth.
   a bad tooth to relieve pain.

2. _____ so that they could win the game.
   to rob a bank of much money.

3. _____ a force that causes the ocean tides.
   pressure on the nerves of the spine.

4. _____ the resources of the country by using less.
   their energy by running slowly at first.

5. _____ herself from the company legally.

6. _____ the family with very strict decisions.
   most famous people with whom he deals.

7. _____ a usually peaceful and unified society.

8. _____ the earth many times before falling.

9. _____ their first efforts to win the election.

10. _____ the works of many famous authors.

11. _____ their efforts to cut down on street crime.

Notice the kinds of words that immediately follow the verb and the kinds of sentence models that fit with certain verbs. You will use these sentence patterns or models to help you write sentences in the next exercise.

Words in Use

Write sentences of your own using the correct form of the verb in parentheses.

1. (conserve) _____

_____

2. (dominate) _____

_____

3. (exert) _____

_____

4. (extract) _____

_____

5. (intensify) _____

_____

6. (launch) _____

_____

7. (scheme) _____

_____

8. (segment) _____

_____

Exercise E
DEFINITIONS AND PARAPHRASES

Select a word or word group from the vocabulary list to complete a paraphrase or definition. Correct choices show that you understand the meanings of the words of the lesson.

Words to Fill the Blanks

acute	edit	launch
barbarian	exert	orbit
conserve	extract	perspective
dissociate from	incident	scheme
dominate	intense	segment

1. (A strong, an extreme, a violent, or an _____) feeling like that of

anger

2. To (pull out, pick out, remove, or _____) seeds from fruit

3. To (start, begin, open, or _____) a drive to raise money

4. Strong animals that (control, stand above, overpower, or _____)

   weaker ones

5. (A circle, a circular movement, a round path, or an _____) around

   the sun

6. To (save, budget, store, or _____) money for later use

7. To (correct, revise, change, or _____) a written report

8. (A severe, a sharp, or _____) illness or pain

9. To (separate from, break away from, untie, or _____) a relationship

   that no longer is suitable

10. A (plan, system, program, or _____) for making money

11. (A savage, an uncivilized one, an uncultured one, a _____) who lives

    much like an animal

12. The (viewpoint, way of seeing, interpretation, or _____) as seen

    through the eyes of another

13. To (try, push with, give, or _____) all your strength

14. (A happening, a situation, an event, or an _____) like an accident

15. One (section, piece, part, or _____) of an orange

LESSON 13

Vocabulary

alter	equilibrium	mobile
appropriate	exclude	phenomenon
commit	horror	reflex
contribute	invade	rely
criticize	miracle	significant

Exercise A

VOCABULARY IN CONTEXT

In the sentences below, the first sentence in each pair, sentence *a*, gives you enough context to make a decision about a general meaning for the vocabulary word in the sentence. After reading sentence *a*, decide whether sentence *b* is true or false. Mark your answer by putting an **X** in the *T* or *F* box before sentence *b*.

1. **a.** Good readers *alter* their reading speeds according to the type of materials being read. Novels and other stories are read fastest.

T ☐   F ☐   **b.** Air conditioning is an example of *altering* your natural environment.

2. **a.** A hammer is the most *appropriate* tool for driving a nail.

T ☐   F ☐   **b.** Many inventions result from the need to find an *appropriate* piece of equipment.

3. **a.** Of all those who *commit* crimes, fewer than 50 percent are finally sentenced to jail.

T ☐   F ☐   **b.** It is possible to *commit* an illegal act without realizing it.

4. **a.** In a group of workers, each person should *contribute* his or her time and talent to whatever the group is trying to do.

T ☐   F ☐   **b.** It is possible to *contribute* your blood to a blood bank.

5. **a.** A good teacher does not simply *criticize* a student for incorrect work. The good teacher also offers advice and opportunity for the student to improve.

T ☐   F ☐   **b.** Some people make a living by *criticizing* the work of others.

107

6. a. Ballet dancers are trained to keep their *equilibrium* even while spinning around many times during the dance.

T ☐ F ☐   b. The paths of the moon and earth in relation to the sun illustrate the state of *equilibrium* of the forces of gravity among three heavenly bodies.

7. a. The definition of "mammals" includes all those animals that nurse their babies and *excludes* animals that do not.

T ☐ F ☐   b. A sign which reads "Females *excluded*" means that all males are to be left out.

8. a. Most nations have learned that they must continually work together to avoid the *horror* of another war.

T ☐ F ☐   b. Fear is associated with *horror*.

9. a. When bacteria *invade* the body, the result is either sickness or a bodily reaction that fights off disease.

T ☐ F ☐   b. When a country has been *invaded*, outsiders have come into that country.

10. a. A *miracle* is a happening that seems to be against the laws of nature and science; it cannot be explained.

T ☐ F ☐   b. *Miracles* are the true foundation of science.

11. a. The modern army is completely *mobile*; it can be moved from place to place in a very short time.

T ☐ F ☐   b. A *mobile* library is a library on wheels.

12. a. An earthquake, like a volcanic eruption, is a natural *phenomenon*.

T ☐ F ☐   b. All natural *phenomena* are dangerous to human beings.

13. a. Because of a *reflex*, or automatic action, the pupil of the eye gets smaller in light and larger in darkness.

T ☐ F ☐   b. Your heart beat is a *reflex* action.

14. a. We can generally *rely* on our families to help us during a time of emergency.

T ☐ F ☐   b. One of the requirements of living in a modern, civilized society is that we must *rely* on one another for our everyday needs.

15. a. If gold can be found in *significant* amounts in an area, it is worthwhile to invest money in mining machinery.

T ☐ F ☐   b. History is a record of *significant* events.

Exercise B
ANALOGIES

Choose a word from the list on the right to complete the analogy. Write the word you have chosen in the blank provided. You will *not* use three of the 18 words in the list.

1. Passion is to excite as horror is to _____   balance

2. Animal is to zebra as phenomenon is to _____   trust

3. Talking is to controlled as reflex is to _____   scare

4. Singular is to plural as appropriate is to _____   automatic

5. Steal is to rob as exclude is to _____   sell

6. Perform is to duties as commit is to _____   improper

7. Evil is to good as significant is to _____   praise

8. Moisten is to dry as criticize is to _____   movement

9. Polish is to shine as invade is to _____   money

10. Accident is to tragic as miracle is to _____   divide

11. Size is to largeness as equilibrium is to _____   unexplainable

12. Differ is to contrast as rely is to _____   change

13. Farm is to crops as contribute is to _____   omit

14. Destroy is to ruin as alter is to _____   typhoon

15. Future is to time as mobile is to _____   wheels

enter

unimportant

crime

Exercise C

WORD FORMS: DERIVATIONS

Complete the following table by writing in the correct forms of the words in the table. Suffixes have been provided for you. The underline before each suffix indicates the number of letters you need to spell the correct, complete derivation. Be sure to put a letter over each dash. Derivative forms that do not change from the base forms, and those that have unusual spellings, are written out for you over the dashes.

Noun Form	Verb Form	Adjective Form	Adverb Form
1. _ _ _ _ _ ation	alter		
2. _ _ _ _ _ _ _ _ _ _ ness		appropriate	_ _ _ _ _ _ _ _ _ _ _ ly
3. _ _ _ _ _ _ ment	commit		
c o m m i t tee			
c o m m i s s i o n			

Noun Form	Verb Form	Adjective Form	Adverb Form
4. _ _ _ _ _ _ _ _ ion	contribute		
5. _ _ _ _ _ _ ism c r i t i c	criticize		
6. _ _ _ _ _ sion _ _ _ _ _ siveness	exclude	_ _ _ _ _ sive	_ _ _ _ _ _ _ _ _ ly
7. horror	_ _ _ _ ify	_ _ _ _ ible	_ _ _ _ _ _ ly
8. _ _ _ _ _ er _ _ _ _ sion	invade		
9. miracle		_ _ _ _ _ ulous	_ _ _ _ _ _ _ _ _ _ ly
10. _ _ _ _ _ ity	mobile		
11. phenomenon p h e n o m e n a (pl.)		_ _ _ _ _ _ _ _ al	
12. reflex	r e f l e x		
13. _ _ _ iance _ _ _ iability	rely	_ _ _ iable	_ _ _ _ _ _ ly
14. _ _ _ _ _ _ _ _ _ ance	_ _ _ _ ify	significant	_ _ _ _ _ _ _ _ _ _ _ ly

Use words from this table to fill the blanks in the next exercise.

Sentence Completion

Use the table of derivation forms you have completed to fill the blanks in this exercise. Use the noun, verb, adjective, or adverb form, depending upon the meaning of the sentence. The sentence numbers correspond to the numbers of the word groups in the table.

1. When you are buying clothes that do not fit properly, the merchant will usually make _____ so that the clothes are made larger or smaller for you.

2. Some psychologists believe that hitting a child is not _____ punishment for the child's bad behavior.

3. A _____ is often appointed to investigate a particular problem and to report its findings to a larger group.

4. The development of x-ray techniques has been one of the great _____ to the science of medicine.

5. Although _____ is often considered negative, it can also be positive in bringing about changes for the better.

6. The _____ of women from the voting population was considered proper in many countries at the beginning of the century.

7. Perhaps new equipment and better regulation can help avoid the _____ tragedies of passenger airline crashes.

8. High fever may result from the _____ of the body by bacteria.

9. The scientific progress of the last 20 years would be considered _____ by people of the last century if they could come back to see it.

10. Low-cost air travel to all parts of the world has greatly increased the _____ _____ of the world's population.

11. A natural _____ such as an earthquake or a hurricane is still beyond the control of modern science.

12. The strength and speed of body _____ may depend upon the general health of the body.

13. Weather experts are continually searching for more _____ means of predicting daily weather.

14. World events of greatest _____ are those that have the greatest effects upon people and places.

Exercise D

WORD ASSOCIATIONS: COLLOCATIONS

Choose subject-verb patterns to make complete, grammatical, and meaningful sentences. Write a *complete subject-verb pattern* in the blank before each word group. Each subject-verb pattern should be used in one of the blanks.

Subject-Verb Patterns

They altered	It horrified
You must commit	They invaded
She contributed	You can rely
He criticized	This signifies
The rules excluded	

1. _____ all persons who were over 70 years old.
   anyone who did not get a score over 85.

2. _____ the spectators to see such an accident.

3. _____ the machine to make it work better.
   their ways of living in the new society.

4. _____ that you are fully licensed as a doctor.
   that you have passed all the courses.

5. _____ a student for not finding the error.
   everyone who did not agree with him.

6. _____ no crimes if you want to stay out of jail.
   errors sometimes to learn a lesson.

7. _____ on your friends to help you when needed.
   on the fact that the sun will rise.

8. _____ time, money, and talent to the work.
   the most to help the undeveloped country.

9. _____ Europe in the ninth century.

Notice the kinds of words that immediately follow the verb and the kinds of sentence models that fit with certain verbs. You will use these sentence patterns or models to help you write sentences in the next exercise.

Words in Use

Write sentences of your own using the correct form of the verb in parentheses.

1. (alter)_____

_____

2. (commit) _____

_____

3. (contribute) _____

_____

4. (criticize) _____

_____

5. (exclude) _____

_____

6. (invade) _____

_____

7. (rely) _____

_____

8. (signify) _____

_____

Exercise E

DEFINITIONS AND PARAPHRASES

After reading each of the incomplete phrases, select a word or word group from the vocabulary list to complete a paraphrase or definition. Correct choices show that you understand the meanings of the vocabulary words.

Words to Fill the Blanks

alter	equilibrium	mobile
appropriate	exclude	phenomenon
commit	horror	reflex
contribute	invade	rely on
criticize	miracle	significant

1. To (trust, depend upon, count on, or _____) a friend to help you

2. (A response, an automatic action, a reaction, or a _____), such as a

sneeze or cough

3. To (find fault with, evaluate, blame, or _____) someone who has bad

habits

4. To (give, participate with, assist with, or _____) time and money

5. To (change, make different, modify, or _____) a person through the

   aging process

6. To (do, perform, carry out, or _____) both good and bad actions

7. To (enter, conquer, spread out in, or _____) a neighboring country

8. To (leave out, omit, force out, or _____) those who do not have the

   proper qualifications

9. (Important, meaningful, notable, or _____) events in history

10. (A natural event, an act of nature, a happening, or a _____), which

    may be expected or unexpected

11. (An unexpected happening, an unexpected event, a wonder, or a _____)

    beyond scientific explanation

12. A (movable, easily moved, or _____) object on rollers

13. (A proper, a suitable, a timely, or an _____) saying, such as "thank

    you"

14. A (terror, fear, fright, or _____) upon seeing a terrible event

15. The control that (balance, coordination, evenness, or _____) gives

    you to walk upright

LESSON
14

Vocabulary

accomplish	deny	imply
assure	expose	magnitude
caste	fertile	obligation
correspond	friction	subjective
credible	habitat	virtually

Exercise A

VOCABULARY IN ACTION

In the sentences below, the first sentence in each pair, sentence *a*, gives you enough context to make a decision about a general meaning for the vocabulary word in the sentence. After reading sentence *a*, decide whether sentence *b* is true or false. Mark your answer by putting an **X** in the *T* or *F* box before sentence *b*.

1. a. Students who *accomplish* their objectives best in school are probably those who follow schedules for both study and free time.

T ☐ F ☐   **b.** If you have *accomplished* a goal, you have also succeeded.

2. a. Salespersons might *assure* customers that the dishes they are selling are unbreakable by dropping them on the floor.

T ☐ F ☐   **b.** Giving a customer a guarantee in writing is a way to *assure* the buyer that the product is well made.

3. a. Many societies have a ranking system that puts people into higher *castes* or lower *castes*, which then determines their positions in that society.

T ☐ F ☐   **b.** A *caste* system is not a product of culture but rather one that is determined by nature.

4. a. A, a, and *a* all *correspond* to the first letter of the Roman alphabet.

T ☐ F ☐   **b.** The + *corresponds* to the label "divide."

5. a. Reports of flying objects from outer space are more *credible* if many witnesses see the same object at the same time.

T ☐ F ☐   **b.** A jury's duty is to decide what evidence is *credible*.

6. a. Some religious groups *deny* the theory of evolution and claim that human life began in its present form.

T ☐ F ☐ b. A student presently enrolled in a university has been *denied* admission.

7. a. A photograph is taken when film is *exposed* briefly to light.

T ☐ F ☐ b. Shelters are built in order to avoid *exposure* to the weather.

8. a. Just as *fertile* soil produces large crops, a *fertile* imagination produces many ideas.

T ☐ F ☐ b. Chickens are produced only from *fertile* eggs.

9. a. The brakes of the automobile stop the car because of the *friction* between brakes and wheels and tires and road.

T ☐ F ☐ b. Ordinarily, we light a match by producing *friction.*

10. a. The *habitat* of an animal is the natural environment in which that animal lives.

T ☐ F ☐ b. The human *habitat* on earth is more limited than that of most other single species of animals.

11. a. It is possible to *imply* a meaning that is directly opposite to the literal meaning of the words spoken.

T ☐ F ☐ b. Legal language used in a contract should avoid *implying* anything; all conditions should be stated directly.

12. a. Earthquakes of a *magnitude* strong enough to cause tidal waves have been felt in several parts of the world.

T ☐ F ☐ b. *Magnitude* indicates a measurement of some kind.

13. a. Those who sign a legal contract have an *obligation* to carry out what they have promised.

T ☐ F ☐ b. There is probably no civilized group on earth in which members have no *obligations.*

14. a. A *subjective* report may be filled with the author's opinions and points of view. On the other hand, an objective report is based upon facts and evidence.

T ☐ F ☐ b. In an autobiography we would expect to find highly *subjective* writing.

15. a. *Virtually* every normal human being begins to talk during the first 1½ years of life, but occasionally a normal child doesn't fit that pattern.

T ☐ F ☐ b. *Virtually* every person classified as Caucasian speaks English as his or her first language.

Exercise B

ANALOGIES

Choose a word from the list on the right to complete each analogy. Write the word you have chosen in the blank provided. You will *not* use three of the 18 words in the list on the right.

1. Message is to **communication** as habitat is to _____ goal

2. Fatigue is to **working** as friction is to _____ opinion

3. Informative is to **explanation** as **subjective** is to _____   confidence

4. Sense is to **taste** as **obligation** is to _____   uncover

5. Frighten is to **scare** as **expose** is to _____   rank

6. Helpful is to **harmful** as **credible** is to_____   agreement

7. Fearless is to **bravery** as **fertile** is to _____   unbelievable

8. Insult is to **irritation** as **assure** is to_____   offer

9. Contribute is to **money** as **deny** is to _____   permission

10. Shout is to **loud** as **imply** is to_____   conceal

11. Forever is to **endless** as **virtually** is to _____   production

12. Achieve is to **success** as **accomplish** is to _____   rubbing

13. Ocean is to **sea** as **caste** is to _____   indirect

14. Surprise is to **amazement** as **correspond** is to _____   size

15. Form is to **shape** as **magnitude** is to _____   possible

debt

environment

nearly

Exercise C
WORD FORMS: DERIVATIONS

Complete the following table by writing in the correct form of the words in the table. Suffixes have been provided for you. The underline before each suffix indicates the number of letters you need to spell the correct, complete derivation. Be sure to put a letter over each dash. Derivative forms that do not change from the base forms, and those that have unusual spellings, are written out for you over the dashes.

Noun Form	Verb Form	Adjective Form	Adverb Form
1. _ _ _ _ _ _ _ _ _ _ ment	accomplish		
2. _ _ _ _ _ ance	assure	_ _ _ _ _ _ d	_ _ _ _ _ _ _ ly
3. _ _ _ _ _ _ _ _ _ ence	correspond		_ _ _ _ _ _ _ _ _ _ ingly

Noun Form	Verb Form	Adjective Form	Adverb Form
4. _ _ _ _ _ ility		credible	
5. _ _ _ ial	deny		
6. _ _ _ _ _ ition	expose	_ _ _ _ _ itory	
7. _ _ _ _ _ _ ity _ _ _ _ _ ization	_ _ _ _ _ _ ize	fertile	
8. friction		_ _ _ _ _ _ _ _ al	
9. _ _ _ _ ication	imply	_ _ _ _ icit	
10. habitat _ _ _ _ _ ation <u>ı n h a b ı t a n t</u>	<u>ı n h a b ı t</u>		
11. obligation	<u>o b l ı g e</u> <u>o b l ı g a t e</u>	_ _ _ _ _ atory	
12.		subjective	_ _ _ _ _ _ _ _ _ _ ly
13.		virtual	_ _ _ _ _ _ _ ly

Use words from this table to fill the blanks in the next exercise.

Sentence Completion

Use the table of derivative forms you have completed to fill the blanks in this exercise. Use the noun, verb, adjective, or adverb form, depending upon the meaning of the sentence. The sentence numbers correspond to the numbers of the word groups in the table.

1. People who write realistic autobiographies—books about themselves—write not only about

   _____ but also about failures.

2. No one has complete _____ of a good life, but working hard toward that goal increases the possibility.

3. There seems to be a direct _____ of both physical and psychological characteristics between humans and the great apes.

4. Someone who is known to tell lies or who cannot be trusted has lost his or her _____ _____ .

5. Anyone who wishes to make a _____ of any connection with a crime would choose to say "not guilty" if brought to trial in court.

6. In many college composition courses, students are taught to write _____ _____ papers that explain or make clear their ideas.

7. Frequently, women who take _____ drugs to help them have children give birth to twins and even triplets.

8. In machines with moving parts, oil is used to cut down on _____ forces between the parts, thereby cutting down on heat and wear.

9. Being able to "read between the lines" means that a reader is able to understand the _____ _____ meaning in the writing.

10. World population figures show that nearly 4½ billion people _____ the earth.

11. Unlike most other animals, human beings are _____ to spend more than a decade raising their young.

12. Scientists attempt to arrive at decisions on the basis of evidence that is as free from _____ _____ opinions as is humanly possible.

13. Identical twins are _____ the same person in two bodies.

Exercise D
WORD ASSOCIATIONS: COLLOCATIONS

Choose subject-verb patterns from the list to make complete, grammatical, and meaningful sentences. Write a *complete subject-verb pattern* in the blank before each word group. Each subject-verb pattern should be used in one of the blanks.

Subject-Verb Patterns

You can accomplish	Farmers fertilize
They assured	This letter implies
It corresponds	These birds inhabit
They denied	We are obliged
They exposed	

1. _____ to carry out the duties of the committee.
to be responsible for our children.

2. _____ that we have 30 days to pay the bill.
but does not say directly that this car is new.

3. _____ their fields to get better, larger crops.

4. _____ many things through hard work.
the life goals you have set for yourself.

5. _____ an island in the South Pacific Ocean.
nearly every country in temperate zones.

6. _____ having anything to do with the crime.
that they owed us the money they borrowed.

7. _____ the meat to the sunlight to dry it out.
the dishonest politician in the newspaper.

8. _____ their parents that they would not be late.
us that our airline seats were available.

9. _____ to the fourth letter of the alphabet.
with the other evidence we found.

Notice the kinds of words that immediately follow the verb and the kinds of sentence models that fit with certain verbs. You will use these sentence patterns or models to help you write sentences in the next exercise.

Words in Use

Write sentences of your own using the correct form of the verb in parentheses.

1. (accomplish) _____

_____

2. (assure) _____

_____

3. (correspond) _____

_____

4. (deny) _____

_____

5. (expose) _____

_____

6. (imply) _____

_____

7. (inhabit) _____

_____

Exercise E

DEFINITIONS AND PARAPHRASES

After reading each of the incomplete phrases, select a word or word group from the vocabulary list to complete a paraphrase or definition. Correct choices show that you understand the meanings of the words of the lesson.

Words to Fill the Blanks

accomplish	deny	imply
assure	expose	magnitude
caste	fertile	obligation
correspond to	friction	subjective
credible	habitat	virtually

1. The (place of living, home, environment, or _____) of certain animals

2. To (refuse, reject, turn down, or _____) a request

3. To (convince, promise, or _____) a buyer by giving a written guarantee

4. To (show, open, leave uncovered, or _____) that which was hidden from view

5. To (match, relate to, correlate with, or _____), as the number 3 with the word "three"

6. To (suggest, hint, say indirectly, or _____) as poets do in their poetry

7. To (succeed in, finish, complete, or _____) the work toward your objective

8. An imagination that is (rich, able to produce, creative, or _____)

9. (Nearly, almost, practically, or _____) everyone needs friendship

10. (A personal, an individual, an opinionated, or a _____) point of view toward a topic

11. (A duty, a responsibility, a debt, an _____) like that of being a parent

12. The (rubbing, scraping, scratching, or _____) of one piece of metal on another

13. The (size, importance, power, or _____) of a volcanic eruption

14. The (rank, class, level, or _____) in a society

15. A (believable, possible, likely, or _____) story

LESSON 15

Vocabulary

derive	inverse	perceive
devote	invest	protest
domain	legislate	quote
heredity	migrate	restrict
interpret	notion	trait

Exercise A

VOCABULARY IN CONTEXT

In the sentences below, the first sentence in each pair, sentence *a*, gives you enough context to find a general meaning for the vocabulary word in the sentence. After reading sentence *a*, decide whether sentence *b* is true or false. Mark your answer by putting an **X** in the *T* or *F* box before sentence *b*.

1. a. Whether vitamins are *derived* from organic or inorganic materials, their chemical reactions in the body are the same.

T ☐ F ☐ b. Modern languages are *derived* from ancient languages.

2. a. After people retire, they usually *devote* more time to hobbies and recreation.

T ☐ F ☐ b. It would not be unusual for a person to *devote* one-third of his or her life to sleeping.

3. a. Today's women are active not only in the *domain* of the home, but also in the *domain* of business.

T ☐ F ☐ b. The study of physics belongs in the *domain* of the sciences.

4. a. *Heredity* largely determines our physical characteristics and our intelligence levels through combinations of genes from our parents.

T ☐ F ☐ b. Blue eyes and blond hair are products of *heredity*.

5. a. In diagnosing a disease the skilled doctor can *interpret* the symptoms of a patient.

T ☐ F ☐ b. The signs and symbols used in mathematics allow all mathematicians to *interpret* them in the same way, regardless of the language they speak.

123

6. a. The alphabet in *inverse* order starts with "Z" and ends with "A."

T ☐ F ☐   b. "Opposite" means about the same as *inverse*.

7. a. There is never a shortage of ideas for new business projects, but there is usually a shortage of people who are willing to *invest* money in these new ideas.

T ☐ F ☐   b. It is possible to *invest* your time as well as your money.

8. a. It is the duty of Congress to *legislate* new laws whenever there is a need for them.

T ☐ F ☐   b. The statement "You can't *legislate* ethics" means that lawmaking should be left to the legislators.

9. a. North American wild geese *migrate* north in spring and south in autumn.

T ☐ F ☐   b. Many plants have the means to *migrate*.

10. a. Many inventions start with the *notion* that there is a better way to do a job.

T ☐ F ☐   b. Most educated people would subscribe to the *notion* that man was created about 2,000 years ago.

11. a. Magicians perform tricks that seem impossible because those watching cannot *perceive* what is really happening.

T ☐ F ☐   b. You probably *perceive* much less than you actually see and hear.

12. a. The average citizen *protests* against high prices of goods but also asks for higher wages, which creates the circle of inflation.

T ☐ F ☐   b. *Protesting* of most kinds is illegal nowadays.

13. a. When an author is *quoted* in a speech, the speaker should use the exact words of the author.

T ☐ F ☐   b. When radio or TV announcers use the words "quote" and "unquote," they mean that they are using the exact words of someone else.

14. a. In dieting to lose weight the dieter is generally *restricted* to eating small amounts of certain kinds of food.

T ☐ F ☐   b. In our society only children have *restrictions* on their social behavior.

15. a. One of the human *traits* that we admire most is honesty.

T ☐ F ☐   b. A person's personality is made up of the set of *traits* that we associate with that person.

Exercise B
ANALOGIES

Choose a word from the list on the right to complete each analogy. Write the word you have chosen in the blank provided. You will *not* use three of the 18 words in the list.

1. **Hear** is to **sound** as **quote** is to _____   acquire

2. **Observe** is to **watch** as **migrate** is to _____   oneself

3. **Rescue** is to **victim** as **devote** is to _____   southern Europe

4. **Agree** is to **contract** as **protest** is to _____   understand

5. **Eat** is to **restaurant** as **invest** is to _____   inherit

6. Steer is to **navigation** as interpret is to _____ explanation

7. Pour is to **liquid** as legislate is to _____ prisoner

8. Automobile is to **Ford** as domain is to _____ reverse

9. Need is to **necessity** as inverse is to _____ characteristic

10. Method is to **system** as notion is to _____ stock market

11. Pet is to **cat** as trait is to _____ law

12. Possess is to **own** as derive is to _____ travel

13. Reward is to **winner** as restrict is to _____ theory

14. Maturity is to **mature** as heredity is to _____ misunderstand

15. Raise is to **lower** as perceive is to _____ sell

complaint

words

kindness

Exercise C

WORD FORMS: DERIVATIONS

Complete the following table by writing in the correct forms of the words in the table. Suffixes have been provided. The underline before each suffix indicates the number of letters you need to spell the correct, complete derivation. Be sure to put a letter over each dash. Derivative forms that do not change from the base forms, and those that have unusual spellings, are written out for you over the dashes.

Noun Form	Verb Form	Adjective Form	Adverb Form
1. _ _ _ _ _ ation	derive		
_ _ _ _ _ ative			
2. _ _ _ _ _ ion	devote	d e v o u t	_ _ _ _ _ _ dly
_ _ _ _ _ ee			
3. heredity	i n h e r i t	_ _ _ _ _ _ _ ary	
i n h e r i t a n c e			
h e r i t a g e			

Noun Form	Verb Form	Adjective Form	Adverb Form
4. _ _ _ _ _ _ _ _ ation	interpret	_ _ _ _ _ _ _ _ ive	
5. _ _ _ _ _ _ ion	<u>invert</u>	inverse	_ _ _ _ _ _ _ ly
6. _ _ _ _ _ _ ment	invest		
_ _ _ _ _ _ or			
7. _ _ _ _ _ _ _ _ ion	legislate	_ _ _ _ _ _ _ _ ive	
_ _ _ _ _ _ _ or			
_ _ _ _ _ _ _ _ ure			
8. _ _ _ _ ant	migrate	_ _ _ _ _ _ ory	
_ _ _ _ _ _ ion			
<u>immigrant</u>			
<u>immigration</u>			
9. <u>perception</u>	perceive	_ _ _ _ _ _ able	
10. <u>protest</u>	protest		
11. _ _ _ _ ation	quote		
12. _ _ _ _ _ _ _ _ ion	restrict	_ _ _ _ _ _ _ _ ive	

Use words from this table to fill the blanks in the next exercise.

Sentence Completion

Use the table of derivative forms you have completed to fill the blanks in this exercise. Use the noun, verb, adjective, or adverb form, depending upon the meaning of the sentence. The sentence numbers correspond to the numbers of the word groups in the table.

1. By now you are familiar with various word forms called _____, which

_____ from base words.

2. In the military services, individuals are given medals and ribbons for their _____

_____ to duty.

3. There is some question as to whether mental illness is a _____ disease

or one that comes through environment.

4. In the United States the final _____ of the Constitution, or the funda-

mental U.S. laws, is the job of the Supreme Court, nine judges appointed by the President

with Senate approval.

5. If we _____ the fraction 1/2, we have 2/1 or the whole number 2.

6. Most _____ are meant to be long-term deals that return steady inter-

est; however, some _____ make money in the stock market in a very

short time.

7. Lawmaking, or _____, is a continual process in most countries, since

new laws and changes in old ones are required regularly.

8. _____ birds seem to be able to return in the spring to the exact local-

ity they left in the fall, and often they return to the same nest.

9. The _____ of color requires a visual sense that most people have, but

some normal humans are "color blind."

10. A strike by union workers who are dissatisfied with their employer is a kind of legal _____

_____.

11. "God helps those who help themselves" is a _____ from a publication

by Benjamin Franklin, an American.

12. _____ on hunting and fishing during certain seasons are made to pre-

vent various wildlife species from dying out through overkilling by humans.

Exercise D

WORD ASSOCIATIONS: COLLOCATIONS

Choose subject-verb patterns to make complete, grammatical, and meaningful sentences. Write a *complete subject-verb pattern* in the blank before each word group. Each subject-verb pattern should be used in one of the blanks.

Subject-Verb Patterns

They derive	The congress legislated
The parents devoted	Birds migrate
The children inherited	You can perceive
People can interpret	The lawyer protested
You can invert	The officials restricted
They invested	The politician quoted

1. _____ from place to place regularly.

2. _____ many of the parents' characteristics.
   brown eyes and black hair.

3. _____ new regulations for immigrants.

4. _____ pleasure from being kind to others.
   aluminum from an ore called bauxite.

5. _____ the difference only in a strong light.
   the changes brought on by old age.

6. _____ the decision of the court.
   the fact that women were not eligible.

7. _____ fractions in some problems.

8. _____ the prisoners to a small yard outside.
   noncitizens from voting in the election.

9. _____ the words of a famous poet.
   directly from Lincoln's speech.

10. _____ most of their time to raising the family.
    themselves to the family business.

11. _____ the same language in different ways.

12. _____ their life savings in the project.

Notice the kinds of words that immediately follow the verb and the kinds of sentence models that fit certain verbs. You will use these sentence patterns or models to help you write sentences in the next exercise.

Words in Use

Write sentences of your own using the correct form of the verb in parentheses.

1. (derive) _____

_____

2. (devote) _____

_____

3. (inherit) _____

_____

4. (interpret) _____

_____

5. (migrate) _____

_____

6. (perceive) _____

_____

7. (restrict) _____

_____

8. (quote) _____

_____

Exercise E
DEFINITIONS AND PARAPHRASES

After reading each of the incomplete phrases, select a word or word group from the vocabulary list to complete a paraphrase or definition. Correct choices to fill the blanks show that you understand the meanings of the vocabulary words.

Words to Fill the Blanks

derive	inverse	perceive
devote	invest in	protest
domain	legislate	quote
heredity	migrate	restrict
interpret	notion	trait

1. To (complain about, object to, disapprove of, or _____) a new law

2. To (give oneself to, contribute, dedicate, or _____) time for helping people

3. To (get, obtain, bring out, or _____) oil from a coconut

4. To (hold down, stop, keep in check, or _____) the rising rate of crime

5. To (give money to, give time to, put work into, or _____) a good business project

6. (A belief, a theory, an idea, or a _____) that you cannot prove

7. To (explain, make clear, translate, or _____) a message in a foreign language

8. The (area, field of work, or _____) of nuclear science

9. To (understand, know, sense, or _____) that you have the answer

10. Senators elected to (make laws, pass rules, regulate, or _____)

11. Things (reversed, turned around, opposite, or _____), like plus (+) and minus (−)

12. The process of (passing on characteristics, inheritance, transmission, or _____ _____) that gives us hair or eye color

13. To (say the exact words of, repeat, refer to, or _____) what someone has said

14. To (move, travel, shift, or _____) from place to place

15. (A quality, a characteristic, an attribute, or a _____) like tallness or honesty

Alphabetical List of Base Words Found in Lessons

Words are identified by lesson numbers.

abandon, 9
accelerate, 8
accomplish, 14
accurate, 10
acquire, 7
acute, 12
adapt, 8
adhere, 1
administer, 7
aggression, 7
agitate, 6
allude, 6
alter, 13
anecdote, 6
annex, 2
antithesis, 5
appropriate, 13
aristocrat, 1
arouse, 4
assemble, 8
assert, 3
assure, 14
atmosphere, 9
attain, 5
attribute, 11

awe, 6
barbarian, 12
bourgeois, P
capitalist, P
caste, 14
category, 7
cease, 4
cell, 7
census, 5
charter, 9
circumstance, 8
clergy, 10
clot, 5
coalesce, P
cohesion, 10
collapse, 7
collide, 6
commit, 13
commune, 5
conceive, 5
condense, 4
conduct, 8
confer, 2
configuration, 1
confirm, 7

conflict, 8
conform, 11
consent, 8
consequence, 9
conserve, 12
console, 6
constitute, 7
contagious, 7
contend, 11
contradict, 6
contrary, 4
contribute, 13
convene, 6
convert, 7
correlate, 1
correspond, 14
credible, 14
criterion, 10
criticize, 13
decline, 8
deduce, 3
deity, 6
delinquent, 7
denounce, 5
dense, 3

deny, 14
derive, 15
devastate, 6
device, 7
devote, 15
dictate, 9
dimension, 9
diplomat, 7
dispute, 2
dissociate, 12
dissolve, 9
distinct, 9
divine, 5
doctrine, 11
domain, 15
domestic, 10
dominate, 12
edit, 12
elaborate, 6
elated, 8
embryo, 1
emit, 4
empirical, 1
enumerate, 1
equate, 1

131

equilibrium, 13
err, 4
ethics, 11
ethnic, 2
evolve, 2
exclude, 13
execute, 7
exert, 12
expose, 14
external, 11
extract, 12
fertile, 14
filament, 5
fragment, P
friction, 14
frustrate, 11
fuse, 3
gene, 4
grant, 11
habitat, 14
heredity, 15
heresy, 6
hibernate, 6
horror, 13
hypothesis, P
imperative, 2
imply, 14
impulse, 2
incident, 12
incline, 11
inert, 8
infect, 11
infer, 4
instinct, 3
intense, 12

interpret, 15
intuition, 10
invade, 13
inverse, 15
invest, 15
investigate, 5
kin, 1
launch, 12
legislate, 15
liberal, P
litigate, P
luster, 1
magnitude, 14
metaphysics, P
metropolis, 3
microbe, 10
migrate, 15
miracle, 13
mobile, 13
molecule, P
momentum, 4
morale, 2
nebulous, 5
niche, 6
norm, 3
notion, 15
obligation, 14
orbit, 12
oscillate, P
parasite, 4
parliament, 3
partition, 2
perceive, 15
persist, 3

perspective, 12
phase, 10
phenomenon, 13
pragmatic, 8
precede, 2
precise, 3
premise, 3
prevail, 4
proceed, 9
proclaim, 4
proposition, 9
prosperous, 1
protest, 15
quote, 15
radical, 9
rational, P
rebel, 4
reflex, 13
regime, 4
reign, 2
reinforce, 9
rely, 13
repress, 8
respond, 9
restore, 8
restrict, 15
retain, 2
reveal, 5
revise, 4
revive, 2
revolt, 1
rhythm, 8
rural, 10
scheme, 12

sect, 3
secular, 5
seek, 9
segment, 12
segregate, 1
sift, 2
significant, 13
skeleton, 10
skull, 3
soluble, 6
spectrum, 8
sphere, 11
spontaneous, 5
stable, 11
stereotype, P
strata, 10
subjective, 11
subordinate, 7
substantial, 11
subtle, 3
successor, 10
suffice, 1
suppress, 3
sustain, 5
synthetic, 9
testify, 10
torture, 2
trace, 10
trait, 15
transcend, 1
treaty, 10
vacate, 11
velocity, 11
virtually, 14